100s
of Fun Things to
Make and Do

100s
of Fun Things to Make and Do

Susie Johns

p

This is a Parragon book
This edition published in 2005

Parragon
Queen Street House
4 Queen Street
Bath BA1 1HE, UK

Copyright © Parragon 2002

Designed, produced and packaged by
Stonecastle Graphics Limited

Text by Susie Johns
Craft items and cookery by Susie Johns
Edited by Gillian Haslam
Designed by Sue Pressley and Paul Turner
Photography by Roddy Paine

ISBN 1-40544-303-0

Printed in China

Disclaimer
This book is fun and will provide many
hours of inspiration for children of all ages.
Safety is very important. Young children
should always be supervised by a
responsible adult when making the craft
items or food and drinks described in this
book. Care should be taken with scissors,
knives and other sharp objects and before
commencing with any project you are
advised to ensure the worksurface is
protected. Always read the instructions
supplied with paints and dyes etc., as they
may differ from those given in this book.
The publisher and their agents cannot
accept liability for any loss, damage or
injury however caused.

Contents

Toys and Games

Introduction

Home-made toys and games are double the fun – fun to make as well as being fun to play with. Here are some new ideas and some variations on traditional favourites, all easy to make.

A load of old junk!

It is surprising what you can create with things that may just be lying around the house. Make a point of collecting together cardboard boxes, including shoe boxes with separate lids, scraps of paper and card, pieces of fabric and felt, dried beans or rice, plastic bags, plastic bottles, string and knitting yarn, paper clips and rubber bands, canisters from cocoa or curry powder, old newspapers – and even odd socks and gloves!

You may need to buy a few things such as soft toy stuffing and bells – but the chances are you will be able to get hold of all the other stuff for free. Just ask around! Build up a box full of basic materials that can be used in all your creative projects. These will include paints and brushes, glue, sticky tape, scissors, needle and thread, ruler, pens and pencils.

A helping hand

If you follow the instructions carefully, and refer to the pictures of the finished projects, you should have no trouble at all in making any or all of the items featured in *Toys and Games*.

Occasionally, if you get stuck, you may have to ask someone for help. You are certainly advised to seek adult assistance when it comes to tricky techniques such as cutting a hole in thick cardboard, where a craft knife may be more useful than a pair of scissors. Or when it comes to sewing, an adult may have more experience and will be able to give you some tips.

Here are some basic tips and techniques to refer to if you get stuck...

Papier mâché

By mixing glue and paper you can produce a hard-wearing shell that will stand up to hours and hours of play. Papier mâché is usually built up on some kind of framework, such as a cardboard model. Construct the framework from pieces cut from a strong cardboard box, holding it all together with plenty of sticky tape.

Dilute some PVA glue with water – just pour some glue into a plastic cup or a jam jar and add an equal amount of water. Stir it well and you should have a mixture resembling thick cream or milk shake. If it is too thick, you can always stir in a little more water.

Brush this mixture all over your model, then apply pieces of newspaper, torn into strips. If the cardboard you have used for the basic construction is thick and sturdy, you should only need to cover it with about three layers of paper and glue to make the finished model nice and strong.

Sometimes papier mâché is built up on a flimsier base. For instance, if you use a balloon as your basic shape, you will need to build up at least seven or eight layers of glue and paper because, once the balloon is burst, the papier mâché shell needs to be really strong and thick, or it will become dented or may even crumple and collapse.

Sewing

All the stitching in these projects is simple. Even if you have not done much – or any – sewing before, it should not be too difficult.

If, however, you don't like sewing, some items, such as the finger puppets, can simply be glued together. Use a special fabric glue or PVA glue, spread very thinly so it does not soak into the fabric or felt.

Paints

The models pictured in *Toys and Games* have been painted with acrylics. You can use poster paints, if you already have these. However, you may have to varnish your painted model to protect it. Use a water-based varnish or simply brush with the same PVA and water mixture you used for the papier mâché. This will dry to a transparent, slightly shiny, protective finish which will make the item more hard-wearing.

Acrylic paints are recommended, however, as they are easy to use, colourful and will give a good finish to your models, without the need for varnishing. Try them if you haven't done so already!

9

Fabric Juggling Balls

These are easier to catch than a ball as they don't roll away. If you are learning to juggle, make a set of three.

You will need:
fabric scraps
needle and thread
dried beans, rice or lentils

1 Cut the fabric scraps into 10cm squares.

2 Place two squares of fabric, in contrasting colours, together, and sew along three sides, approximately 5mm from the edges.

3 Turn right sides out and pour in dried beans, lentils or rice until bags are three-quarters full.

4 Fold in raw edges on the open side. Place folded edges together and stitch the opening closed.

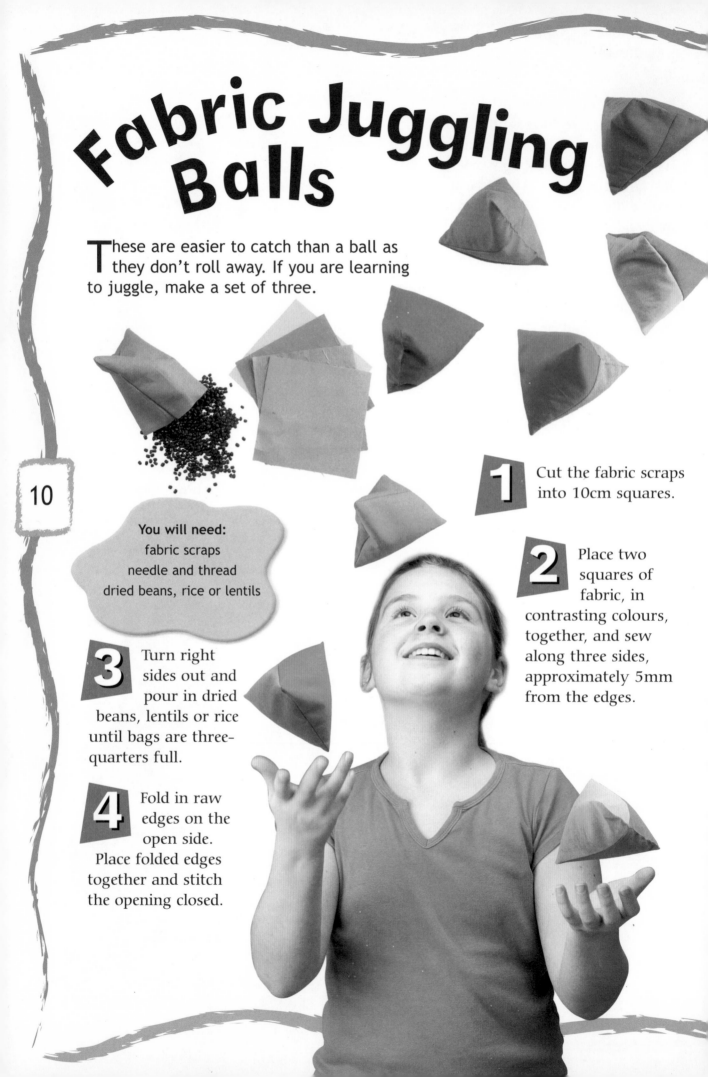

Bean bag people

As with the fabric juggling balls, you will need fabric scraps. Cut two identical shapes for the head and body. It helps to draw the shape of your bean bag person on paper first. When you are satisfied with the shape, cut it out and use it as a template for cutting fabric. Stitch the fabric for the head to the body fabric, then with wrong sides facing outwards, stitch the front and back together. Leave a small gap so you can turn it right sides out. Fill three-quarters full with beans or lentils and stitch the opening closed. Draw features on the face with a permanent marker pen.

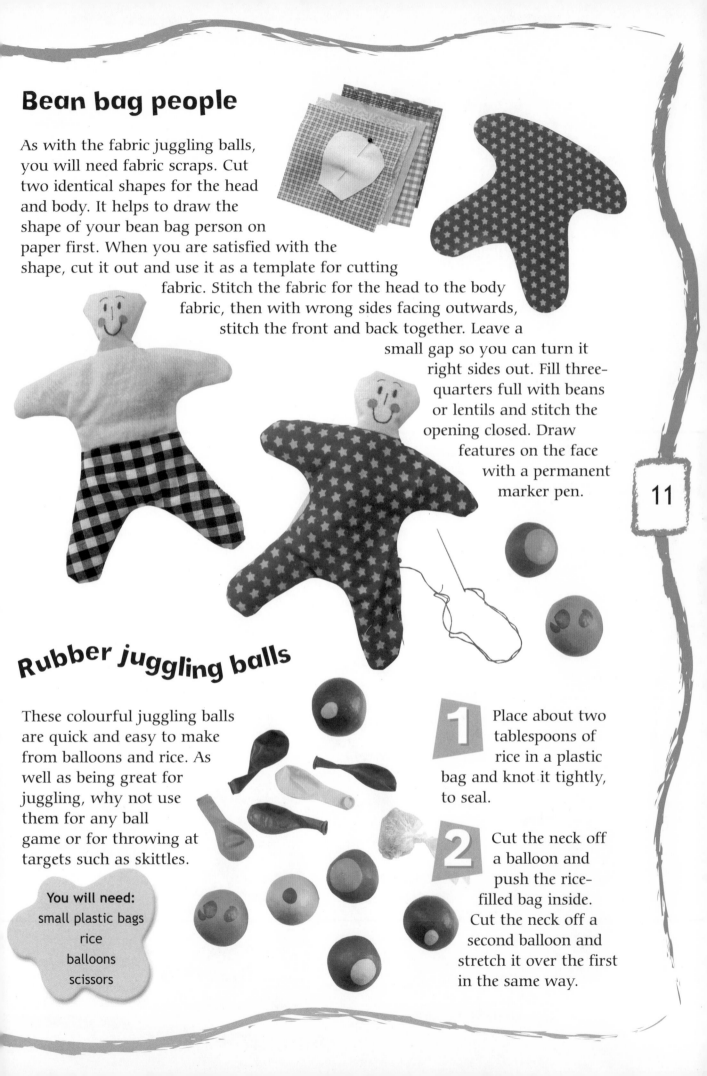

11

Rubber juggling balls

These colourful juggling balls are quick and easy to make from balloons and rice. As well as being great for juggling, why not use them for any ball game or for throwing at targets such as skittles.

You will need:
small plastic bags
rice
balloons
scissors

1 Place about two tablespoons of rice in a plastic bag and knot it tightly, to seal.

2 Cut the neck off a balloon and push the rice-filled bag inside. Cut the neck off a second balloon and stretch it over the first in the same way.

Puppet Parade

If you have made a puppet theatre, maybe you would like to make some actors to perform in it? Paint a wooden spoon with a happy/sad face, customise an odd glove into a furry monster, or create a whole cast of finger puppet characters to act out your favourite stories.

Finger puppets

You can make all kinds of finger puppet characters: kings and queens, angels, sailors, or even Father Christmas. All you need are scraps of coloured felt, a needle and thread and lots of imagination.

You will need:
coloured felt
scissors
needle and thread

1 Using the puppets pictured here as a guide, cut out shapes for bodies, hands, feet and other features. The body can be a simple rectangle – place your finger on a piece of felt and draw around it, then add a bit extra all round so it will fit once it has been stitched. Or you can add arms to the basic shape.

2 Choose which piece will be the front part of the body then stitch on head, hands and other details.

3 Stitch the front part of the body to the back, leaving the bottom edge open so you can fit your finger inside.

Wooden spoon puppet

Paint a face on a wooden spoon. To make a two-sided puppet, paint a face on each side – one happy and one sad, perhaps? Cut out two identical tunic shapes from felt or fabric and stitch together leaving a gap at the neckline and along the bottom edge, so the wooden spoon's handle fits inside. Apply a little glue to the inside neck of the tunic to fasten it to the wooden spoon.

Glove puppet

Stitch the three middle fingers of a glove together. Do this by stitching up the sides of the fingers – you will still need to get your hand inside.

Cut out a face from felt and stitch to the glove. Once again, take care not to stitch right through the fingers. Add details cut from felt and hair made from a piece of feather trim.

Traditional Games

Test your powers of concentration and your strategic skills with a game of draughts, chess or tic tac toe. But before you do – why not make your own game board and counters, so you can also show off your creative ability!

Draught/chessboard

This board is simply made from the lid of a large cardboard box. If you cannot find a suitable lid, you could cut the base from a cardboard box, leaving a small rim all round, or simply paint a large sheet of cardboard. The counters pictured are made from wooden discs. You could just as easily use painted bottle tops or circles cut from cardboard.

You will need:
large cardboard box lid or sheet of cardboard
white emulsion paint (optional)
acrylic paints
paintbrushes
ruler and pencil
32 wooden or cardboard discs
coloured paper
PVA glue

1 Paint the inside of the box lid with white acrylic or emulsion paint. When dry, measure and mark out the squares for the board and paint them in your choice of colours. The board needs to be eight squares by eight squares.

2 Paint half the discs one colour and half a contrasting colour. When the paint is dry, cut out shapes from paper and glue them on to one side of the counters, to make chess pieces. Leave the other side of each counter blank, for playing draughts.

3D noughts and crosses

Otherwise known as tic tac toe, this game is usually played with pencils and paper. This papier mâché version is not only fun to play with, but also fun to make from scraps of cardboard and newspaper.

You will need:
cardboard
ruler
scissors
sticky tape
PVA glue
newspapers
10 wooden or cardboard discs
acrylic paints
paintbrushes

1 Cut eight strips of card measuring 18cm x 1.5cm. Form four strips into a grid, fixing them together with sticky tape where they overlap. Add a second layer of strips on top, binding them tightly to the first layer with sticky tape, to form a rigid base.

2 Dilute PVA glue with a little water and brush all over the cardboard base, then apply torn strips of newspaper, winding them round to cover the edges of the card and brushing with more diluted PVA. Build up about three or four layers of newspaper in this way, then leave to dry.

3 Meanwhile, paint five discs one colour and the other five a contrasting colour and leave to dry. Paint a cross on top of five of the disks and a nought on the other five.

4 Paint the papier mâché grid, using any colour you like. You may wish to outline the edges in black or a contrasting colour. Leave to dry.

15

Target Games

Fun to play on a rainy day or great for a party. Enjoy constructing and painting these simple games – and then enjoy playing them!

Aunt Sally

Here is a table-top version of an old fairground game that is easy to make from a single piece of card and can be stored flat, so will take up very little space. Copy the face or make up your own – a clown, perhaps, or an animal such as a lion?

You will need:
cardboard box
ruler
scissors
acrylic paints
paintbrushes

1 Cut a rectangle measuring 50cm x 20cm from a cardboard box, making sure that a fold runs across it, about 20cm from one of the shorter ends, to form a hinge. This 20cm square forms the base.

2 Draw a face with a big mouth on the larger portion of the cardboard. Cut out the mouth and paint the face using acrylic paints. Paint the reverse of the card, too.

3 To play the game, place a bowl or cup on the shorter end of the card and prop the larger portion against it. Throw crumpled balls of paper at the target, aiming for the mouth, and decide how many points to award for every ball that lands in the cup.

Tiddlywinks

This is quick to make, fun to play and pocket-sized so you can carry it with you.

1 Cut a 10cm square of thick card. Draw a star shape with a circle in the centre. Paint the design or use paper cutouts stuck on to the card.

2 Place a small cup or bottle top in the centre then, using a large tiddlywink to press and flick the smaller counters, aim for the cup.

3 Decide on a scoring system – 5 points for landing on the star and 10 points for getting the tiddlywink into the cup, perhaps?

Target box

1 Draw a series of circles, like a target, on the lid of a shoe box.

2 Cut out the centre circle and paint the other rings in different colours, using acrylic paints.

3 Paint on numbers, or cut these out from paper and stick in place.

4 Lie the box flat and throw crumpled balls of paper or kitchen foil, aiming for the hole in the centre but scoring points for any balls that land on the numbered rings.

Gone Fishing

Make a shoal of paper fish, then try to catch them with a home-made fishing rod. You can put a magnet on the end of your fishing line or a hook – it's up to you.

You will need:
metallic silver card
poster paints
paintbrush
scissors
paperclips
wooden stick
string or cord
magnet or paperclip

18

Crafty tip
To play the game, place the fish in a box lid or plastic bowl – or why not cut a pond shape from corrugated card?

1 Paint the card with a layer of thick poster paint in one or two colours. Before the paint is dry, use the other end of the paintbrush to scratch fish shapes. Leave to dry.

2 Cut out the fish shapes and attach a paperclip to each one.

3 Tie a length of string to one end of the stick. Tie a magnet or a paperclip bent into a hook at the other end of the string.

Flying fish

This Japanese-style kite is simply made from tissue paper and string. Perfect for a breezy day, it is

probably too delicate to fly in very strong winds.

You will need:
tissue paper
coloured inks
plate
very wide brush or sponge
fine paintbrush
glue stick
paper scraps
hole punch
string

1 Place sheets of tissue paper on a layer of newspaper. Pour a little ink on to a plate, dip in the brush or sponge and brush stripes of colour across the tissue paper. Leave to dry.

2 Use paint and a fine brush to paint a fish shape on one sheet of tissue paper, and details such as fins and scales. Leave to dry then place this upside down under a second sheet of tissue and draw another fish, this time in reverse, for the other side of the kite.

3 With the glue stick, draw a thin line of glue all around the edge of one of the fish, on the reverse side. Do not apply glue to openings at mouth and tail. Place this sheet on the second sheet, matching up the fish outlines, press down and, when the glue is dry, cut out.

4 Cut four small squares of paper and glue them back to back on each side of the fish kite's mouth. Punch a hole in each one and thread with a short length of string, tying one end to each hole. Tie the end of a longer length of string to the centre of the first piece.

Character Skittles

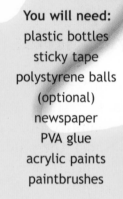

S ave empty plastic bottles from soft drinks to make a set of skittles. Here are four funny characters but you could make as many as you like. For indoor play, use a soft ball to try to knock them over.

You will need:
plastic bottles
sticky tape
polystyrene balls
(optional)
newspaper
PVA glue
acrylic paints
paintbrushes

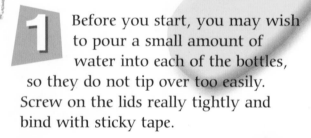

1 Before you start, you may wish to pour a small amount of water into each of the bottles, so they do not tip over too easily. Screw on the lids really tightly and bind with sticky tape.

2 Glue a polystyrene ball to the top of each bottle. If you do not have any, just crumple a sheet of newspaper into a tight ball and use this for the head.

3 Dilute some PVA glue with water to the consistency of thick cream and brush all over the bottle and the ball. Cover with torn newspaper strips – at least four layers but preferably five or six, to make the skittles really tough.

4 When the papier mâché is dry, paint the skittles, using your imagination to create funny faces and costumes.

Can skittles

Save canisters from coffee, drinking chocolate and savoury snacks. Paint them with brightly coloured acrylic paints, adding painted numbers for scoring. Stack up the cans and try to knock them down by throwing a ball at them. Score the appropriate number of points for every can you knock over.

Music Makers

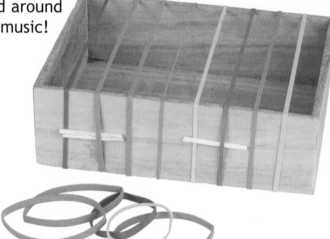

You don't need to be a maestro – with a collection of bits and pieces found around the house, you can make marvellous music!

Box guitar

For an instant guitar, stretch rubber bands over a box. You could use a cardboard shoe box or chocolate box, or a small wooden box. To adjust the sound of each string, try inserting some matches. To play the guitar, pluck the strings with your fingertips.

Milk bottle xylophone

Part fill clean milk bottles with water. Add a few drops of food colouring, if you like. If you arrange eight bottles in a row and adjust the water levels carefully, you can produce a musical scale and play tunes.

Drum sticks

Push one end of a wooden stick into a large wooden bead. Make a pair of sticks and decorate them with acrylic paints, then use them to tap out tunes on your milk bottle xylophone.

Maracas

If you like salsa music, here is the very thing for you – a pair of colourful maracas that you can shake to the rhythm.

Crafty Tips
You can fill these shakers with rice, dried beans, crumpled balls of kitchen foil or paper clips. Try different things for a different sound.

You will need:
2 cardboard tubes
2 balloons
PVA glue
newspapers
string
rice, beans or lentils (see Crafty tips)
acrylic paints
paintbrushes

1 Cover the cardboard tubes with three layers of papier mâché. To do this, brush the tubes with PVA diluted to the consistency of thick cream and add torn strips of newspaper. Leave aside to dry.

2 Meanwhile, pour some rice into each balloon, then inflate and knot the end. Cover each balloon with at least six or seven layers of papier mâché. Attach a length of string to each one and hang up to dry.

3 When the papier mâché is dry, burst the balloons and remove them from the papier mâché shells. Push one end of each tube into a balloon and add two more layers of papier mâché to cover the join. Leave to dry.

4 Paint the maracas in colourful designs.

23

Soft Toys

Scraps of fabric, needle and thread and some soft stuffing are all you need to make a collection of cuddly toys. Use fabrics that are nice to touch, such as natural cotton or soft velvet and practice your sewing skills.

Fabric ball

This squashy ball is soft enough for indoor play. Made from scraps of colourful cotton fabric, stitched together and stuffed with a soft filling, it's easier to make than you might think, and safe enough for a toddler, but do not give it to a baby.

You will need:
pieces of cotton fabric, at least
25cm x 15cm
needle and thread
polyester stuffing
rattle (optional – see Crafty tips)

1 Enlarge templates A and B to twice their size (or larger). This is easy to do on a photocopier. Use them to cut out shapes from fabric. You will need four of shape A and eight of shape B.

2 Stitch together one shape A and two shapes Bs, to make a segment. Repeat until you have four segments. With each one, leave a gap for stuffing, stuff firmly and stitch the opening closed.

Crafty tips
To add an extra dimension to your ball, put a rattle inside when you are stuffing one of the segments. To make a rattle, place a few beads or dried beans, or a small bell, inside a plastic film canister.

24

Flat cat

Cut two identical cat shapes from velvet. On one, stitch on eyes, ears and nose cut from coloured felt. With black thread in your needle, stitch a mouth shape. Now, with the velvety sides of the fabric together, stitch all round, leaving a small gap so you can turn your cat inside out. Push stuffing through the gap, then sew the gap closed. To give the cat jointed arms and legs, stitch across through all thicknesses of fabric.

You will need:
pieces of velvet
needle and thread
polyester stuffing

3 Stitch two of the segments together, by joining the pointed ends. Do the same with the other pair but at the same time, join the ends to the top and bottom of the first pair. To hide these joins you can tie a length of ribbon around the ends. Do not give the ball to a baby.

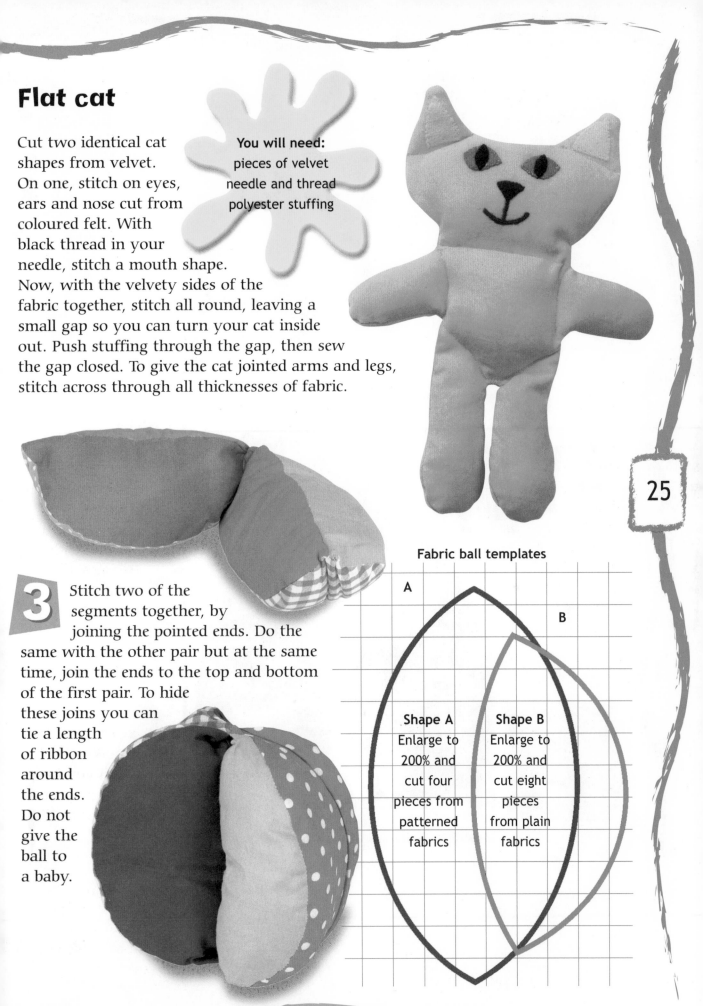

Fabric ball templates

A

B

Shape A	Shape B
Enlarge to 200% and cut four pieces from patterned fabrics	Enlarge to 200% and cut eight pieces from plain fabrics

25

Art Gallery

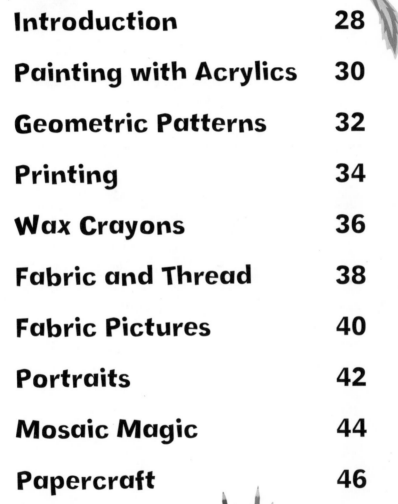

Introduction

Everyone has the ability to draw. Being good at it just takes a bit of practice! And there are lots of ways to make pictures, besides painting and drawing – *Art Gallery* will show you how! Arm yourself with pencils, paper, paint and glue and be prepared to make some marvellous pictures!

If you are stuck for picture-making inspiration, there are plenty of ideas to get you going on the following pages. But once you have mastered some of the techniques, remember that there is subject matter all around you. Create pictures of your family, your house, your pets, your possessions, or make patterns and shapes.

Use pencil and paper, or paint, or have a go at printing. Or get really stuck in with glue and make a collage with fabrics, or scraps of coloured and textured papers and cardboard. You could even use needle and thread to stitch a picture – it's up to you! It's fun to be creative.

Paper bank

Recycling makes sense when it comes to making artwork. Envelopes, letters, catalogues, newspapers and magazines are all useful. And look out for more unusual paper and card: packaging often includes good quality cardboard as well as acetate panels; after a day's outing you may have a pocketful of tickets and maps; save wrappers from sweets, and all the crinkly papers from inside a chocolate box; hoard scraps of tissue paper, greaseproof paper, kitchen foil and corrugated card; and ask friends and family for interesting pieces of fabric and felt.

Crafty tips

You can buy special acrylic paper, available in single sheets or pads, from art shops. This is the best paper to use, as its surface has been specially treated. Or use pieces of cardboard, cut from a cardboard box, and paint it on both sides with a layer of emulsion paint before you start painting with acrylics.

Drawing materials

In your pencil case or tin, keep a few pencils, a rubber and sharpener, a black marker pen and a fine tipped black felt pen. A ruler is useful, too.

Then a basic set of coloured pencils is great for sketching. When birthdays and Christmas come around, you could ask for a wider selection of coloured pencils, or maybe some oil pastels, a box of water colour paints and some pads of good quality drawing paper.

Use your pocket money to buy wax crayons. You will also need some sticky tape and glue, for sticking.

Sticking tips

As you experiment with collage, you will find you need different types of glue for sticking different things.

A glue stick is great for all kinds of paper and cardboard. PVA glue will stick bulkier things – even pieces of wood and plastic – but you may need to use quite a lot and leave plenty of time for it to dry. Fabric glue is best for most fabrics, especially thin ones, as it will not soak through or stain – but use it in a very thin layer. Glitter glue is great for sticking sequins and beads and adds an extra touch of sparkle!

29

Painting with Acrylics

One of the brilliant things you can do with acrylic paints is to blend colours together; another is overpainting one colour on top of another, and then there's the thickness of the paint which allows you to build up interesting textures. Try these projects and test the special qualities of acrylics for yourself.

You will need:
acrylic paper or cardboard
acrylic paints
paintbrushes
black paper
scissors
glue stick

Paint a firework picture

This involves blending paints to produce an atmospheric background, with a bit of overpainting to create very effective fireworks.

1 Paint three bands of colour – blue, purple and orange – and brush the edges of each colour with a dry brush to blend colours together.

2 When the background is dry, paint starburst fireworks with pale colours such as pink, yellow and pale blue, using a fine brush, then add dots of white paint.

3 Finally, cut out a skyline of buildings from black paper and, when your painting is dry, stick it in place along the bottom edge, using a glue stick.

How to paint a 3D space rocket picture

This picture is created by overpainting several colours. The rocket is painted separately and flies above the background surface, creating a 3D effect.

You will need:
acrylic paper or cardboard
pencil
ruler
acrylic paints
paintbrushes
glue stick
matchbox

1 With pencil and ruler, draw a rectangle on a sheet of paper or board. This is your picture area. Draw a circle, to represent a planet.

2 Paint the circle pale blue and the background a dark blue – almost black. Leave to dry.

3 To make the planet look more realistic, paint patches of blue in different shades to represent sea and land.

4 Paint multicoloured stars in the sky. To do this, make a blob of paint and, with the other end of your paintbrush, pull out lines of paint all round.

31

5 Paint a rocket on a separate piece of paper or board. When dry, cut it out. Using a glue stick, attach a matchbox to the background and stick the rocket on top.

Geometric Patterns

You don't need any special equipment to produce patterns on paper – these were made with a potato! Ask an adult to help you cut potatoes into shapes and make sure you cover your work surface with plenty of newspaper as potato printing can be very messy.

Safety tip

It is best to cut the potato with a sharp kitchen knife. Ask an adult to do this for you. A single potato can be used to make several different patterns – just slice off the pattern you have just made, to produce a clean surface, and start again.

You will need:
potatoes
knife (see safety tip)
acrylic paints or poster paints
paintbrush
paper

1 Cut potatoes into simple shapes. Brush the surface with paint, not too thick.

2 Press the painted surface of the potato on to a sheet of paper. Repeat the print in a regular pattern all over the paper.

3 If you like, add a second shape when the first is dry.

Printing a brick wall

Cut a piece of potato into a rectangle. Using several shades of orange and brown paint, brush the surface of the potato with a slightly different mixture of colours each time and print a regular pattern all over a sheet of paper. Why not use the brick pattern as a background for a picture? Or print brick patterns all over a cardboard box, to make a house.

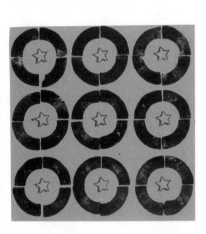

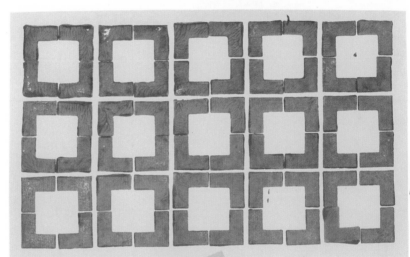

Pattern pictures

Repeat a simple shape to make a picture, like this truck. This is a great way to make cards or party invitations as you can print a number of pictures, all the same.

Printing

The great thing about a print is that you can repeat it and make lots of copies – perfect for invitations or Christmas cards!

How to print a lino cut horse

You will need:
lino
light-coloured pencil
lino-cutting tool
water-based lino printing ink
sheet of plastic
roller
paper

This technique requires a special lino-cutting tool, a piece of special lino, a small roller and some printing ink, all of which are available from art and craft shops.

If you are a newcomer to this craft, start by buying a handle and just two cutters: a pointed v-shaped one for cutting fine lines and details and a scoop-shaped one for cutting away larger areas.

1 Draw a picture on the surface of the lino, using a light-coloured pencil. Remember that, whatever design you draw, it will be reversed when you print it.

2 Cut away the parts of the design that you do not wish to print. The areas that you cut away will not be covered with ink and so the paper will show through.

3 Squeeze out a little ink on to a sheet of plastic. You can use a piece of acetate, or a plastic bag stretched out and attached to your work surface round all edges with masking tape. Roll out the ink until the roller is evenly covered, then roll it across the surface of the lino until it is covered with a thin film of ink.

4 Place a sheet of paper on top of the lino and rub gently all over, to press the ink on to the paper. Carefully peel away the paper and leave to dry.

5 You can apply more ink to the lino and make as many prints as you wish. To produce a multicoloured effect, simply squeeze blobs of two or more colours on to the plastic and roll carefully so the roller picks up stripes of the different colours.

Leaf prints

Coat leaves with paint, using a brush or roller, then press on to paper. Different leaves will give different results – try choosing ones with prominent veins. Print an all-over pattern of leaves or cut out individual leaf prints to make greetings cards or gift tags.

Wax Crayons

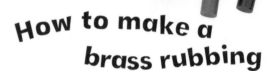

Crayons are not just for little kids. Their waxy texture makes them perfect for all kinds of special techniques, from rubbings to wax resist! Try some of these...

You will need:
large sheets of paper
dark-coloured, chunky
wax crayons

How to make a brass rubbing

Objects with a raised texture can be used to make interesting pictures. You place a piece of paper on top, rub all over with a crayon and the patterns are reproduced as if by magic! Brass plaques can be found in many churches and are an ideal subject for rubbings. You may have to ask permission before you start – and be careful not to mark or damage the precious brasses!

1 Place the paper over the brass plaque. You can weight down the corners of a large sheet with pebbles or other heavy objects.

2 Making sure the paper doesn't slip as you work, rub all over the surface, above the brass, using the side of the crayon. Start gently, making light marks, and build up until the picture becomes darker.

Wax butterfly

Shave wax crayons using a chunky pencil sharpener. Arrange the shavings in a pattern on one side of a folded piece of paper. Fold the paper to enclose the shavings, place inside a sheet of newspaper and press with a hot iron – with the assistance of an adult. When you open out the paper, you will have a symmetrical pattern of melted wax.

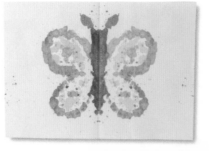

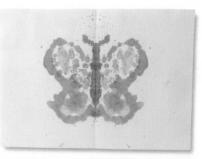

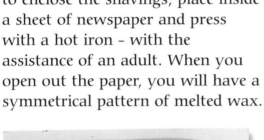

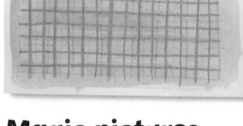

Magic pictures

Wax and water do not mix. Make a drawing on a sheet of paper using a wax crayon. Brush over it with water colour paint. Instead of a crayon, try using a candle – a white candle on white paper produces a 'magic' result!

Fabric and Thread

It was a tradition in the nineteenth century for young children to learn cross stitch. They would practice their skills by making samplers, consisting of rows of alphabet letters and simple pictures, and the cross stitch letters would also be sewn onto clothes and bed sheets, as an identifying mark.

Simple as ABC

Start with this simple sampler, to practice the stitch technique.

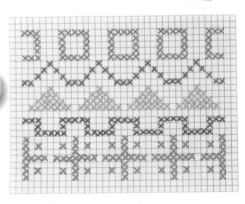

1 Draw out your design on graph paper. Fill in one square with a cross to represent each stitch. You can copy the one from this page or make up your own.

You will need:
graph paper
coloured felt tip pens
cross stitch fabric
embroidery hoop
tapestry needle
embroidery thread
scissors

2 Stretch your fabric in an embroidery hoop. Thread your needle with three strands of thread. At the back of the fabric, run the needle under a few rows of the fabric weave, to hold the end of the thread in place.

3 Bring the needle through one of the holes to the front of the fabric. To make a single cross stitch, push the needle through the hole diagonally opposite the one it has come up through. Then make a second diagonal stitch that crosses over the first.

4 Follow the design you have drawn, making a series of cross stitches to correspond with the ones on the graph.

5 When you have finished stitching, remove the fabric from the hoop and trim it to the size and shape you want. Fray the edges by pulling out some of the threads.

Pattern picture

Have fun designing rows of patterns on your graph paper then translating these patterns onto stitches. Zigzags are easy, so are crosses and squares. By practising your stitches in this way, you will be able to produce a colourful and attractive picture. Stitch a border all around to make it complete.

39

Cross stitch materials

Cross stitch fabric is specially woven to create a grid pattern with holes through which to push your needle and create neat stitches in the form of a cross. The fabric can be finely or coarsely woven. If you are a beginner, choose a coarse fabric, with 10 or 12 holes to 2.5cm of fabric. The sales assistant in the shop will help you.

The needle to use is a tapestry needle, which has a slightly blunt point. Embroidery thread is made up of six strands. Cut a length of thread, then pull out three individual strands and thread these into your needle.

Potted plants

As you become more confident, try designing pictures instead of letters and patterns. It is slightly more challenging but great fun. You could try to copy this picture onto graph paper, or make up one of your own.

Fabric Pictures

One of the best things about making pictures with fabrics is the wide variety of colours, textures and thicknesses available. Collect together as many different scraps as you can: they could be from old clothes you were otherwise going to throw away, or pieces from friends who like to sew.

Fabric picture

Stitching fabric pieces on to a fabric background is known as appliqué. Keep shapes simple and use a variety of coloured fabric scraps to produce a charming, country-style picture!

You will need:
small pieces of fabric
larger piece of fabric, for background
pins
needle and thread
scissors

1 Cut out a variety of shapes from fabrics. Pin them in place on the background fabric.

2 To stitch them in place, fold under the edge and stitch the fold to the background fabric. This is fiddly but quite easy. Make your stitches as small as possible, for a neat finish.

3 Turn under the edges of the background fabric, to neaten them. You can glue the fabric picture to a piece of thick cardboard, to display it if you wish.

Make a felt picture

Felt is great for making all sorts of things and inexpensive to buy. Cut scraps into shapes, keep them in a box, then take them out and make pictures. When you have finished playing, they can go back in the box ready for another day!

1 Cover the shoe box with fabric. Glue a piece of felt inside the lid, to use as a background for your pictures.

You will need:
shoe box
large and small pieces of felt
scissors
glue

2 Cut shapes from felt. Geometric shapes such as squares and triangles are useful for constructing buildings. Circles and strips can be made into trees and people. Use your imagination!

Portraits

If you want to be a serious artist, you will probably want to try your hand at portraiture! But if you can't get anyone to sit still for long enough, don't despair – just use photographs, like other artists do!

Coloured pencil portrait

Coloured pencils are a good medium to start with as they are inexpensive, easy to use, and you can build up your drawing slowly until you are pleased with the result.

You will need:
A4 sheet of good quality
cartridge paper
pencil, preferably 4B
coloured pencils (see tip below)
photograph for reference

Coloured pencils
You do not need many colours to start with. A basic set of 12 coloured pencils is a good starting point, as colours can be mixed on the paper. You may like to try soluble pencils, which are exactly like ordinary coloured pencils with the added bonus that, if you go over your pencil lines with a paintbrush dipped in water, the colour dissolves so it looks like water colour paint!

Pencil portrait

Start with a simple portrait in pencil. Choose good quality cartridge paper, which has a slightly rough, textured surface, and a pencil with a fairly soft lead, such as a 4B. Draw a grid of guidelines on your paper and lay an acetate grid over the photo you wish to copy. Carefully copy the shapes within each square on to the larger squares on your paper. Rub out the grid lines, then add detail.

1 Scale up the photograph to the size you want, using the simple method described below.

2 Once you have sketched the outline of your subject, using pencil, use coloured pencils to add colour and shading. It will not matter if you have not got exactly the right shade of coloured pencil as colours can be mixed. Practice on a scrap of paper, starting with a light colour, shading very gently, then going over this with other colours, again very gently, until you have built up the shade you want.

3 Keep referring to your photograph. You do not have to reproduce every detail – this is your picture and you can change whatever you like and leave things out, if you wish!

Mosaic Magic

By cutting out and sticking down pieces of coloured paper to make pictures and patterns, you can create some very bold, colourful effects. And you don't have to go out and buy coloured paper – use pages from catalogues and magazines, and scraps of wrapping paper.

Clown with rainbow border

You will need:
A4 sheet of coloured paper
pencil
ruler
small scraps of coloured paper
scissors
glue stick

1 Draw a line, a ruler's width, all round the paper, to form a border.

2 Cut coloured paper into thin strips and glue these down to fill the border area with a colourful striped pattern.

3 Cut shapes from coloured paper to make the clown's head, body, legs and so on. Arrange these in the centre of the background, sticking each piece neatly in place.

Mermaid with shiny rainbow border

As well as plain coloured papers, look for shiny, metallic papers. Cut these into strips and make a border, as before. To make the mermaid's tail sparkle and shimmer, glue on masses of sequins, using glitter glue.

How to make a cheerful cockerel collage

Start with a sheet of thick card, larger than A4, as a base and stick on a sheet of A4 coloured paper, to form a background. Cut out shapes from different coloured papers – a body, head, feet, wing and so on – and stick these in place using a glue stick.

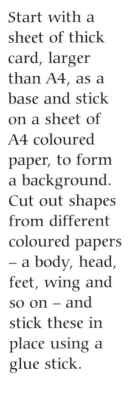

Add a border of mosaic squares and, because this is the most colourful occupant in the hen house, why not add some bright cutout starbursts of coloured paper as a final flourish?

Papercraft

Paper is marvellous stuff! It comes in all kinds of colours and textures, matt or shiny, plain or patterned. Save scraps of paper from other projects, and cut pieces from magazines and catalogues. Keep all your scraps in a box, so you'll have a wide variety to choose from when you want to make a picture.

Coat rack

Customize this design with representations of your own coat and bag, to make a really personal picture.

You will need:
cardboard or thick paper, for background
plain and patterned paper scraps
scissors
glue stick

1 Start by cutting a strip of brown paper to represent the coat rack. Cut a second, smaller strip and stick it on top to make it appear more three-dimensional. Cut circles of paper to represent pegs.

2 Now cut shapes from various coloured and patterned papers, for clothes. Cut a hanger from silver paper, for example, and, to make a pair of trousers to go over the hanger, crease the paper to look like folded fabric.

Dustbin

To make this picture look really three-dimensional, cover a shallow box with grey paper, for the dustbin, then fill with all kinds of bits and pieces such as crumpled sweet wrappers. Make flies from cut-out paper shapes, drawing wiggly flight paths with pen or pencil. Have fun and let your imagination run away with you!

Tile designs

Start with a square of card and play around with colours and shapes: a central star, triangles, squares and dots. When you have stuck down all the pieces, protect the surface by covering with clear self-adhesive film, or by brushing with diluted PVA glue to give a glossy finish.

Cards and Gifts

Introduction

A home-made gift or greeting is not only more special than one you can buy in the shops – it's also likely to be a lot cheaper. With paper and scissors, or fabric and thread, or cardboard, glue and paint, you can make gifts for mums, dads, aunties, babies, friends, teachers – for any person and any occasion!

Whether it's a birthday, an anniversary, a wedding or the birth of a baby, there are plenty of ideas in *Cards and Gifts* to inspire you to make something extra special.

For a quick and easy present, a bookmark or set of personalized stationery can be put together with just some scraps of coloured paper, scissors and a glue stick!

Fabric or paper?

If you want to try your hand at sewing, there are lots of things to make. Choose your fabrics carefully, though. Something that will need a lot of washing should be made from a cotton fabric, which means you will have to neaten raw edges and sew things together firmly so they don't come apart! Felt is easier to stitch but not washable – so it's not suitable for aprons, towels, bibs or anything that will need laundering!

You can make some great gifts from papier mâché – but remember to plan ahead. Paper and glue need time to dry and painting and varnishing can take longer than you think, so remember to take this into consideration!

Ribbons, tapes and trimmings

Ribbon is good for tying things! Collect as many different kinds as you can. They can be made from thin, transparent fabrics, satin, velvet or even paper. Try to gather together different colours and widths. Ribbon is cheaper to buy in markets than in craft shops.

51

Crafty tips
To bind the edge of fabric with bias binding, open up the binding and place one edge level with the raw edge of the fabric. Stitch along the fold, through both thicknesses of fabric. Then fold the binding over the edge of the fabric and, on the other side, stitch down the other folded edge, using neat stitches.

Bias binding is a special kind of folded tape, usually made from cotton, that is extremely useful in sewing projects for covering the raw edges of fabric. Used to edge a baby's bib or a cushion cover, it also provides a nice, colourful border (see box for tips on how to sew).

While you're on the lookout for things to collect together for your work box, save buttons, poppers, zips, lengths of cord, different kinds of threads, pins (glass-headed ones are best, as you can see them easily) and needles of various sizes. Scissors, a tape measure, string, paper, paints and brushes, fabric glue and glitter will also come in useful.

Say it with Flowers

Whatever the occasion, flowers are a good choice for greetings cards. Here are some simple but very eye-catching ideas.

3D flower card

Simple paper cutouts can be given an extra dimension by folding and adding a real ribbon bow to tie up the bouquet!

You will need:
piece of A5 coloured card
scraps of coloured paper
glue stick
small, round stickers
short lengths of ribbon and string
scissors

1 Fold the card in half. Cut green paper into thin strips and glue in place, to make stems.

2 Cut out six-petalled flower shapes from white and yellow card. Pinch each petal between your finger and thumb then, applying a blob of glue to the centre of each flower, stick them in place. Add a small sticker to each flower centre.

3 Make two holes, one either side of the flower stems, thread ribbon through and tie in a bow.

4 Finally, cut a label from a scrap of paper, add a sticker and punch a hole, threading it with string.

Chunky flower cards

Cut simple shapes from thick cardboard – flower pots, stems, leaves and flowers – and paint the front and edges of each piece. When the paint is dry, stick the pieces on the front of a folded card for a really good 3D effect.

Gift Wrapping

Have you got an awkward-shaped gift to wrap? A jar, perhaps, a key ring or even a banana-shaped pen? Here are some bright ideas!

Gift bag

It is easier than you may think to produce a very impressive result. Just follow the steps below.

You will need:
small rectangular box
thick wrapping paper
double-sided sticky tape
hole punch
ribbon
scissors

1 Cut a piece of wrapping paper wide enough to go around the box with a 1cm overlap, and about 3–4cm longer at either end.

2 Wrap the paper around the box and stick the edges together using double-sided tape.

3 At one end of the box, neatly fold in the edges and stick down using double-sided tape, to form the base of the bag.

4 Remove the box. Neaten the top edge by folding it inside, or simply cut it off to the desired height.

5 Make two holes at the front and back, about 1cm from the top, and thread with ribbon, knotting it on the inside to form handles.

Tissue paper straw

Roll up a sheet of tissue paper and flatten it. Cut across into very thin strips. Gather the strips in your hands and crumple slightly, then fluff them out.

Cardboard tube

Save tubes from toilet rolls or kitchen paper! Slip the gift inside, then cut a piece of wrapping paper twice the length of the tube and wide enough to go around it with a 1cm overlap. Wrap the paper around the tube and glue or tape in place. At one end, neatly fold over the paper then cut a circle of paper and glue in place for a neat finish. At the other end, gather the paper and tie with a length of ribbon after putting the gift inside.

Pyramid

Cut a square of card to form the base, then draw four triangles with the same measurement as the square for their base. Apply glue to one side of each piece and place them flat on a piece of wrapping paper with the square in the centre and one triangle on each side. Cut out the paper, about 1cm all round. Fold the paper over and stick in place. Cover with pieces of paper, cut to shape, in a contrasting colour. Punch a hole on the point of each triangle, thread with ribbon, pop a present inside and tie closed.

Baby Gifts

WARNING
Always ask an adult to check that the toy you have made is safe to give to a baby or small child. Remember to ensure there are no buttons or other small items which could cause choking.

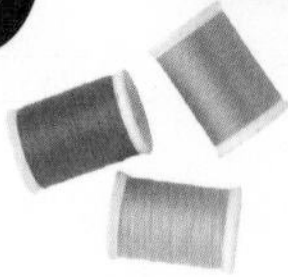

The birth of a baby is always a great occasion. Celebrate by making one of these gifts – very easy even if you are a beginner at sewing – or a card with the baby's name.

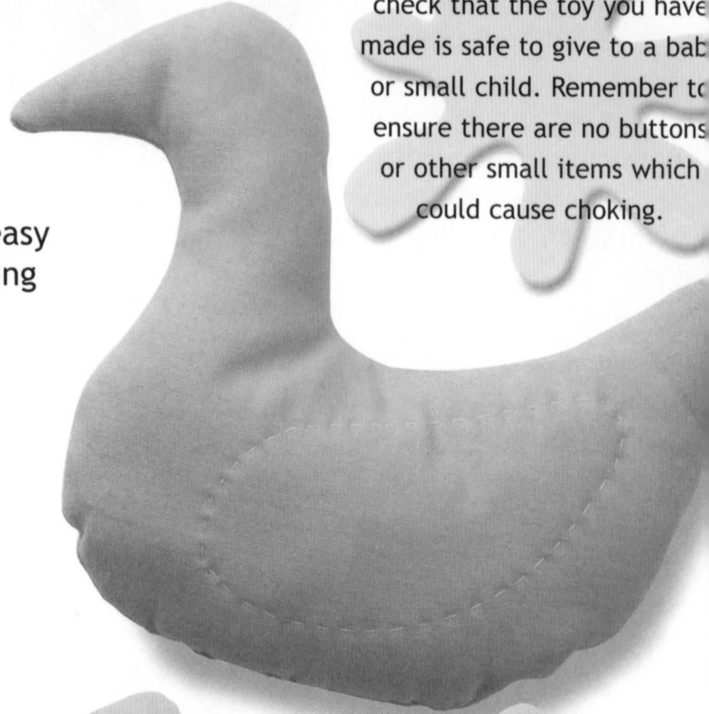

Flat duck

You will need:
pieces of cotton fabric
needle and thread
polyester stuffing

Cut two identical duck shapes from cotton fabric. Put the two shapes together with the right side of the fabric on the inside. Stitch all round, leaving a small gap so you can turn your duck inside out. Push stuffing through the gap, then neatly sew the gap closed.

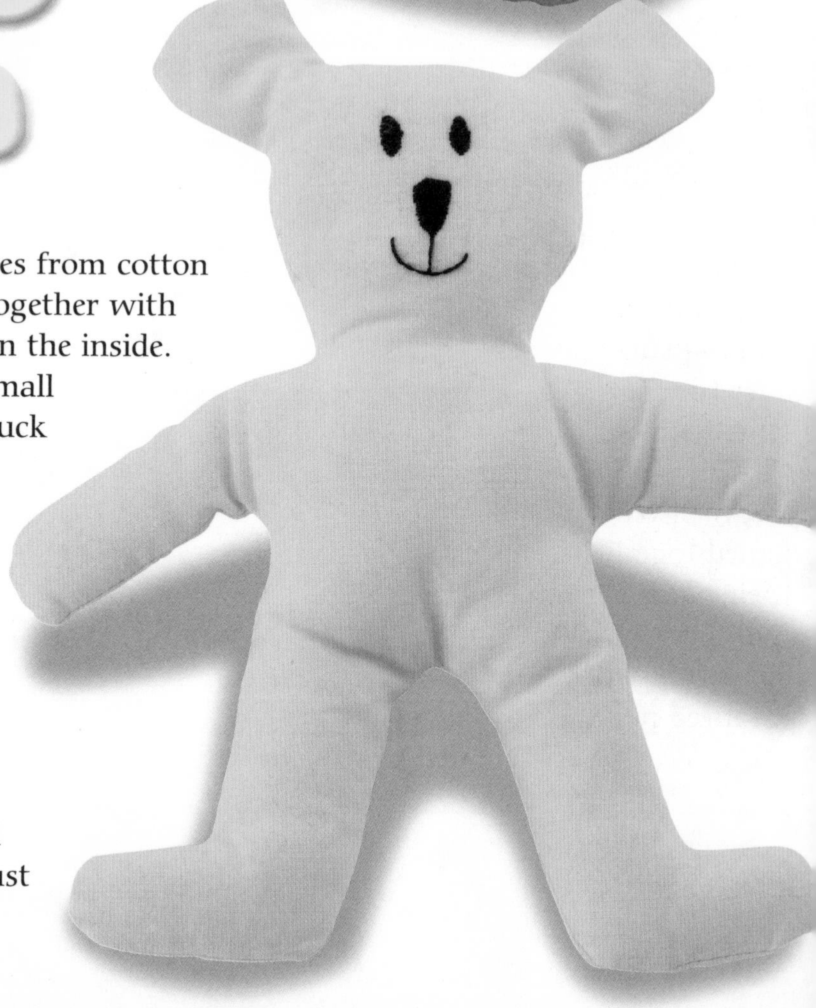

Teddy

This teddy is made, just like the duck from two fabric shapes stitched together and stuffed. Make three bears, just like in the story, or make other animal shapes.

Teddy card

Fold a long strip of thin card in concertina folds. The number of folds will depend on the number of letters in the baby's name. Draw a teddy shape on the top of the folded card, making sure the arms and legs go over the folds. Cut through all layers and open out the card. You should have a row of teddies, joined together by their paws. Decorate with eyes, noses and letters cut from coloured paper.

Presents for Pets

Even pets can get presents! Doesn't your favourite animal deserve a special treat?

Painted pet bowls

Using special paints suitable for decorating china, paint your design – such as a fish bone for a cat – leave it to dry and, following the manufacturer's instructions, ask an adult to bake the dish in a hot oven to set the paint.

Felt mouse

Cut a heart shape from felt, fold in half and stitch all round, leaving a small gap for stuffing. You can stuff it with sawdust or cotton wool, then sew up the opening. Add circles of felt for ears, sewn firmly in place, beady eyes and a tail of plaited wool with a bell on the end.

Pet place mats

Plastic-coated mats are a practical idea as they can be wiped clean – perfect if your cat or dog is a messy eater!

You will need:
sheet of A4 coloured card
scraps of coloured paper
glue stick
clear self-adhesive film

1 Cut a basic cat or dog shape from paper, stick it in place on the sheet of card, then add details, also cut from coloured paper.

2 When you are happy with your design, cover both back and front with clear adhesive film.

59

Crafty tips
Instead of covering your finished picture with self-adhesive film, you could have it laminated. Some photocopy shops or office suppliers offer this service and it gives a really hard-wearing, long-lasting result.

Desk Tidies

Most grown-ups would find these items very useful, on their office desk, or even in the kitchen to keep paper, envelopes and a pen or pencil always to hand! There's even a bookmark to mark a page in the diary!

Stationery folder

Not only is this a nice present for someone – but it should encourage them to write you a thank-you letter!

You will need:
sheet of A4 card
scraps of coloured paper
glue stick
sticky tape
ribbon
stamp or stencil, for decorating envelopes

1 Fold the card in half, then fold in 2cm at either side and 3cm along the bottom. Cut away the corners along the fold lines, then glue the folded-in edges together at the two bottom corners.

2 Cut slits, one on each side, and insert a piece of ribbon into each, securing the ends with a small piece of sticky tape, hidden under the folds.

3 Cut pieces of paper, each 17cm x 12cm, decorating each one with the recipient's name, or a small motif, or both.

Lizard bookmark

Cut a lizard shape from green paper, stick it to black card and cut around the outline again. Add scales cut from paler green paper, and a beady eye! The lizard's front legs slip over the front of the page!

Pencil pot

Choose a container that has no sharp edges. A cocoa or custard powder tin is ideal. Cover the outside with a strips of paper, then cut pencil shapes from coloured paper and stick all round, using a glue stick.

Family Photo Fun

Relatives will love a present with a picture of their favourite grandchild or nephew or niece or other family member. To avoid damaging precious photographic prints, have photocopies made. Black and white ones are cheaper than colour – and very eye-catching!

Photo calendar

Inexpensive calendars – just the days and dates, without any pictures – are available from stationers very cheaply, or you could print out your own, with the help of a computer.

OCTOBER
M	T	W	T	F	S	S
1	2	3	4	5	6	7
8	9	10	11	12	13	14
15	16	17	18	19	20	21
22	23	24	25	26	27	28
29	30	31				

You will need:
empty CD case
small calendar
coloured paper
photocopies of favourite photos
glue stick

1 Cut twelve pieces of coloured paper to fit inside the CD case.

2 Trim photocopies so they are smaller than the coloured paper. Stick one in place on each of the pieces of paper and stick on one calendar month below.

Photo box

Paint a small wooden or cardboard box – from a craft shop or junk shop, perhaps. It looks particularly effective if you paint the box all over in one colour, such as yellow, then, when this is dry, paint a different colour such as turquoise blue, on top. When dry, lightly rub with sandpaper to reveal some of the colour beneath. Stick a favourite photograph on the lid and fill the box with small photos cut to fit.

Photo cube

Cut six equal-sized squares of thin card and join them together with sticky tape, to make a cube. Don't worry if the tape looks untidy – it will be covered up by the pictures! Cut photographs (or photocopies) into squares, the same size as the sides of the cube, and glue in place using a glue stick.

Photo card

Spare photocopies can simply be stuck onto a piece of folded card for a very personal greetings card, suitable for almost any occasion!

Tea Time Treats

The chances are you know someone who really loves a cup of tea! Here is just the right greetings card for them, and a table mat to stand their cup on! And anyone who enjoys cooking would welcome a home-made pot holder.

Coasters

These colourful table mats are just the right size for a cup or glass – but if you are patient and have the time, you could make larger ones.

You will need:
1 metre cord or thick string
scraps of fabric
embroidery thread
needle
scissors

1 Tear the fabric into strips, 3–4cm wide. Place one end of the cord along a strip of fabric, wrap the fabric round and bind with thread. You do not have to be very neat or even.

2 When you come to the end of the fabric strip, add another strip and carry on binding it with thread. From time to time, tie off the end of one piece of thread and start again with a different colour.

3 When you have wrapped the entire length of cord, start coiling it into a tight spiral. Thread your needle with one strand of thread and stitch the edges of the bound cord together as you coil it.

Pot holder

This can be used to hold a hot pot handle or to stand a hot pan on, like a table mat. The layer of wadding inside acts as insulation.

You will need:
scraps of plain and patterned cotton fabric
needle and thread
polyester wadding
bias binding
button
scissors

1 Cut nine 10cm squares from different coloured fabrics. Stitch them together.

2 Cut petal shapes from fabric scraps, pin and stitch in place in the centre of the patchwork. To do this, simply tuck under the raw edges of the fabric and sew to the background, using tiny stitches.

3 Cut a piece of polyester wadding and a piece of backing fabric the same size as your patchwork. Place the backing fabric with the wadding on top and the patchwork on top of the other two and stitch together all round, close to the edges.

4 Then bind the edges with bias binding (see introduction). Add a loop of binding for hanging, and a button for decoration.

Tea pot card

Whoever you send this to can have a greetings card and a real cup of tea!

EARL GREY

Fold a piece of card in half. On the front, cut out and stick down teapot and teacup shapes. Make a slit below the lid of the teapot and slip the string from a teabag through it. Tape the string inside the front of the card, to keep the teabag in place.

65

Winter Warmers

Basic sewing and knitting skills are all you need to complete these colourful projects. If you have never picked up a pair of knitting needles or a needle and thread, maybe now is the time to try?

Hot water bottle cover

Vary the motif according to who it is for – a grandparent, a young child, perhaps, or even your dog! You could even use a different coloured fleece for each side of the cover.

You will need:
hot water bottle
fleece fabric, about 60cm x 40cm
scrap paper
pen or pencil
scraps of fabric
needle and thread
ribbon, about 50cm
scissors

1 Place a hot water bottle on a piece of paper and draw around it, to make a template slightly larger than the bottle itself. Do not draw around the shape of the neck, but continue the sides up in a straight line. You should end up with a sort of rectangle with two rounded corners.

2 Place the paper template on a double thickness of fleece, pin it in place and cut out.

3 Decorate one of the fleece shapes with fabric cutouts. See the baby bibs on 'Baby Gifts' pages for how to do this.

4 With the right sides facing inwards, stitch the two shapes together, about 1cm from the edges all round, leaving the to edge open. Turn right sides out.

5 Stitch two lengths of ribbon to the seams, near the top of the cover. Slip the hot water bottle inside, gather the fabric round the top and tie in place.

Cushion

Follow the instructions given and you should create a cushion measuring 22cm square. Feel free to vary the colours and the widths of the stripes, or to make a larger or smaller cushion simply by casting on more or fewer stitches!

You will need:
25g double knitting yarn in each of 8 colours
4.5mm needles
22cm square cushion pad (see note)
tapestry needle
scraps of card
scissors

67

Note
If you don't have a cushion pad the right size, make one from two squares of fabric stuffed with polyester toy stuffing.

1 Cast on 80 stitches in your first colour (red), then knit 10 rows of plain knitting.

2 Break off the yarn, leaving an end about 20cm long, then continue knitting with your second colour (orange) and knit 10 rows.

3 Break off the yarn and continue with your third colour (yellow). Continue in this way, knitting 10 rows of each colour, until you have completed eight stripes and your piece of knitting is 22cm deep. Cast off.

4 Thread the tapestry needle with one of the loose ends of yarn. Fold the knitting in half and stitch the edges together along two sides. Use the correct colour of yarn to stitch each stripe, for a neat effect. Push the cushion pad in through the open side, then stitch this side closed.

5 Make pom poms to decorate the corners. Draw two 6cm circles on a piece of card, and a 3cm circle in the centre of each. Cut them out. Place these card rings together and wind round and round with yarn. When the rings are covered with a thick layer of yarn, cut the yarn between the outer edges of the rings, slip a length of yarn between the two rings and tie tightly, Slip the rings off, then trim the woolly ball with scissors, to neaten it. Stitch in place.

Needlework

If you know someone who likes to sew, they will welcome one of these home-made gifts. Or, if you are keen on sewing, make one for yourself!

Pin cushion

This is easy to make – just find a suitable lid from an old jar and a scrap of colourful fabric.

You will need:
plastic lid, about 8cm in diameter
scrap of cotton fabric
needle and thread
polyester wadding
fabric glue
pins

1 Cut a circle of fabric about 18cm in diameter.

2 Stitch all around the edge of the fabric with a running stitch. Pull the end of the thread to gather the fabric.

3 Place a generous handful of wadding in the centre of the circle, pull up the thread end tightly and fasten firmly.

4 Apply glue to the inside of the lid, over the base and up the sides. Press the fabric ball into the lid and leave until the glue is dry. Stick in some pins.

Felt needle case

Anyone who is keen on needlework – or has a name tag to stitch or a button to sew on – will find this needle case useful.

1 Cut a piece of fabric 20cm x 15cm. Cut shapes from felt and stitch to the right-hand half of the fabric. This will form the front cover of the needle case.

2 Cut two pieces of card, each measuring 10cm x 7.5cm and place them, side by side, on the wrong side of the fabric, with a small gap in the centre. Fold the edges of the fabric over the card and glue in place. Do not worry if it looks a bit untidy at this stage as the edges of the fabric will be covered.

3 Cut a piece of felt 10cm x 15cm. Place it on top of the card. Cut two lengths of ribbon, each about 20cm long, and place them in between the layers, on either side of the needle case cover. Stitch the felt to the folded edge of the fabric, all round.

4 Cut two pieces of felt, in contrasting colours, each measuring 12cm x 7.5cm. Cut the edges with zigzag scissors, if you have them. Place on top of each other on the felt side of the needle case cover and stitch up the centre, through all thicknesses of fabric. The line of stitching should go up through the gap between the two pieces of card.

You will need:
coloured felt
fabric
fabric glue
cardboard
ribbon
needle and thread

69

Seasonal Fun

Introduction

Valentine's Day, Easter, a wedding, birthday party, Halloween or Christmas – all year round there are special times for being creative. Decorating the house for a party? Get out the scissors, glue and coloured paper and start snipping! Want to impress your valentine? Don't just send a card – make them something special! Whatever the occasion, your efforts will be really appreciated by friends and family!

Materials

Paper and paint, cardboard and glue, sticky tape and scissors will all come in useful for seasonal makes! Save all these in a cardboard box so they are handy whenever you feel like being creative.

Save scraps of paper and card – you never know when you might need them. For the projects in *Seasonal Fun*, coloured card and paper, tissue and crêpe paper are particularly useful, and self-adhesive film, the transparent kind used for covering books, and the more glittery kind, will also be very useful.

Stock up on coloured felt, too. It's available from craft shops and department stores in a wide range of colours. And remember to buy needles, thread and pins, too, for stitching.

Many special occasions call for a touch of glitter and sparkle, so make sure you have lots of glitter glue to hand. Or maybe just plenty of glue and pots of glitter for sprinkling.

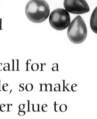

Sequins add a magical sparkle and they come in all sorts of shapes, sizes and colours. Buying them in small pots can be expensive. You may find it better to buy a big bag of mixed sequins. And fake jewels are useful, too. Choose ones with flat backs that can be glued to greetings cards, fabric and models.

There are several papier mâché projects in *Seasonal Fun*. This is an easy craft where you use old newspapers and PVA glue diluted with water (one part glue to one part water is about right, or add more or less water to achieve a consistency like cream) to make fantastic models!

Valentine's Day

February 14th is the time to let someone know how much you love them. You may want to send a card – but these love tokens will last much longer!

Felt heart

Send a felt heart to your Valentine this year, instead of a card. Stitch the initial letter of your name on it and see if they can guess who it is from.

You will need:
coloured felt
needle and thread
beads
polyester toy stuffing
scissors
ribbon

1 Cut two heart shapes from bright pink felt and a larger one, with a fancy edging, from pale pink.

2 Decorate one of the heart shapes by stitching on your initial, cut from felt. Add other felt shapes and stitch on beads.

3 Sandwich the pale pink heart shape between the other two pieces and stitch all round, leaving a small gap. Push a little stuffing inside, to pad out the heart slightly, then finish stitching. Add a loop of ribbon if you like, so the heart can be hung up.

Heart-shaped frame

1 Cut a crown shape from cardboard, then cut a heart-shaped opening in the centre.

2 Cover with two layers of papier mâché (see introduction) and when dry, paint it with a layer of watered-down paint so the newspaper shows through slightly.

3 Cut out words or letters from a magazine and paste them in a random pattern all over, then paint a coloured border.

Heart-throb box

Decorate a heart-shaped card box, from a craft shop, with a photo of your favourite pin-up, adding glitter glue, shiny tape and a sequin or fake jewel.

Mother's Day

Your mum will really appreciate a home-made present on her special day – as well as a cup of tea, of course!

Papier mâché tray

Treat your mum to breakfast in bed on a special, home-made tray, painted with her favourite colours.

You will need:
thick cardboard
sticky tape
newspapers
PVA glue
paints

3 Dilute PVA glue with water to the consistency of pouring cream and brush it all over the tray, then stick on torn strips of newspaper. For a really strong result, build up about four or five layers of papier mâché in this way. Leave to dry.

1 Cut a rectangle of cardboard the size you want your finished tray to be. Use a thick cardboard box – stick two layers together if you don't think it will be thick enough. Cut off the corners of the rectangle to give a rounded shape.

4 Paint the tray in your choice of colours. You could paint a picture of a teapot and teacup, like this one, or perhaps a pattern of flowers?

2 For the edge of the tray, cut a long strip of card, preferably corrugated card so it will bend easily, and stick it all round the edge of the tray base, using sticky tape.

Papier mâché vase

Moulding papier mâché around a balloon makes a strong shell – but don't forget it's made of paper, so you must not put water in it!

You will need:
1 long balloon
newspapers
PVA glue
small scraps of cardboard
sticky tape
paints and brushes

1 Blow up the balloon to the size you want your finished vase to be.

2 Dilute PVA with water and brush it all over the balloon. Cover with torn strips of newspaper. You will need to build up at least eight layers of glue and newspaper – preferably ten – to make a really thick papier mâché shell. Leave to dry.

3 Burst the balloon and remove it. Trim both ends of the papier mâché. Decide which will be the base and cut a circle of card to fit, taping it securely in place. On the neck end, roll up a sheet of newspaper into a sausage and tape this in place to form a rim.

4 Apply three more layers of papier mâché to the base and rim. Leave to dry.

5 Paint the vase, first with a base coat of white, then with your choice of pattern. A flower, perhaps? Or a heart to show your mum how much you love her!

77

Funky flower

As a fun alternative to a fresh flower, this colourful creation can be made in minutes!

You will need:
5 red pipe cleaners
2 yellow pipe cleaners
4 green pipe cleaners

1 Bend each red pipe cleaner into a loop, twisting the ends together, to secure.

2 Place the ends of the red 'petals' together in the centre and twist one end of a yellow pipe cleaner around all of them, leaving the remainder of the yellow pipe cleaner straight, to form the stem. Wrap the second yellow pipe cleaner round and round to form the flower's centre.

3 Loop two green pipe cleaners to form leaves and fold the ends around the stem, then wind the remaining two green pipe cleaners around the stem, securing the leaves in place as you go.

Spring Time

To celebrate the coming of spring, with flowers and new-born lambs – and Easter on the horizon – here are some fun makes, including a container ready to hold some lovely chocolate Easter eggs!

Papier mâché rabbit

Make this bunny to decorate your Easter table, or just as a mascot! The basic shape is moulded on two balloons.

1 Blow up two balloons, quite small. Brush each one with diluted PVA glue and cover with at least eight layers of newspaper, torn into small strips. Hang up the balloons to dry.

You will need:
2 balloons
newspapers
PVA glue
egg box
cardboard
paints
paintbrushes

2 Burst the balloons and, trimming off any excess, glue them together to form the rabbit's body and head.

3 Roll up sheets of newspaper into sausages and tape these in place to form the arms, legs and ears. Stick a cup cut from an egg box on to the front of the head for the nose. Cover the base with a piece of cardboard cut to size.

4 Cover your model with a further three layers of papier mâché and leave to dry.

5 Paint the rabbit, using acrylic paints or poster paints.

Decorated basket

Cut an octagon from cardboard.
Cut eight squares the same measurement
as each side of the octagon and tape in
place using gummed brown parcel tape.
Add a strip of card for a handle. Paint the
basket all over with one colour then paint
flowers all round the edges.
Fill with shredded tissue and
tiny chocolate Easter eggs.

Shredded tissue

Roll up a sheet of tissue paper and
flatten it. Cut across into very thin
strips. Gather the strips in your hands
and crumple slightly, then fluff them
out and you have tissue paper straw!

Easter chicks

Cut the body shape from cardboard,
plus a triangle to make the feet.
Glue the two together and cover
with three layers of papier mâché.

When dry, paint the chick
yellow with an orange beak
and feet, adding details with
a black marker pen.

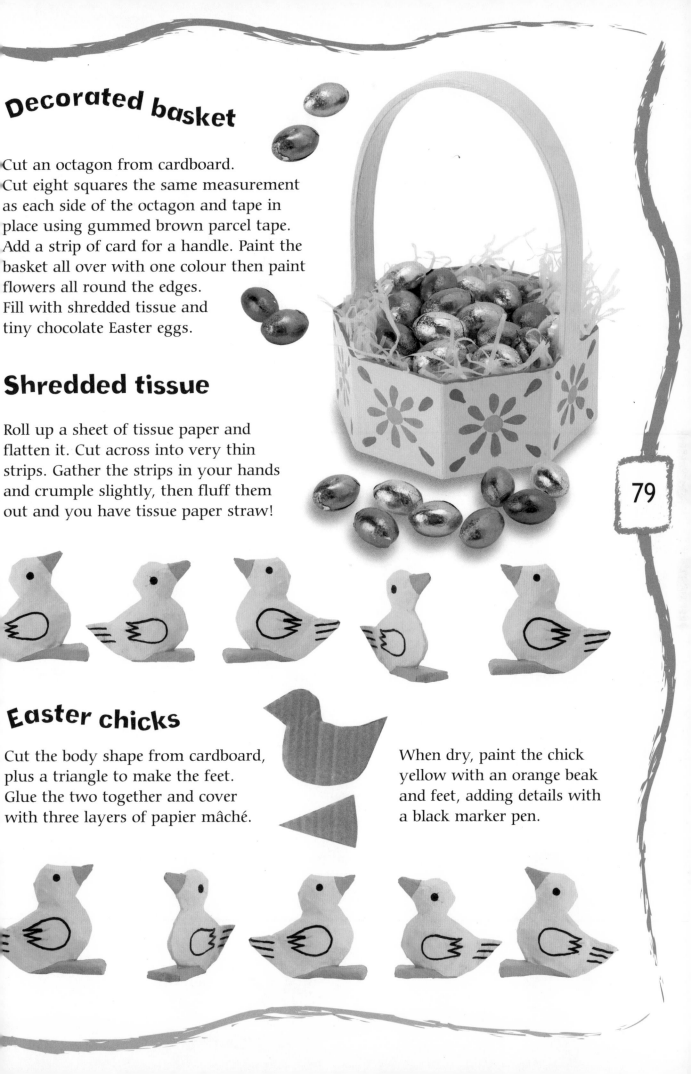

Easter Eggs

Even before the invention of chocolate eggs, decorated eggs were part of the Easter celebrations. You can colour eggs, ready to eat, or make more lasting decorations from hollow egg shells.

Painted egg cups

Easter weekend is the first big holiday of the year. Dress up the breakfast table with home-made egg cups and felt covers to keep your boiled eggs nice and warm! You can buy wooden egg cups from craft shops – or look in junk shops or charity shops and you may pick one up at a real bargain price!

1 If the wood has been varnished, rub it with sandpaper before you paint it.

2 Use a bright colour all over, then add spots and stripes in contrasting colours.

Painted eggs

Empty egg shells make a long-lasting Easter decoration that you can put away and take out year after year.

1 Make a hole at each end of a fresh egg, using a drawing pin, then put your mouth over one of the holes and blow out the contents into a bowl.

2 Wash the egg, inside and out, dry it, then paint with acrylic paints.

Cress eggheads

Save egg shell halves instead of throwing them in the bin! Wash, draw a face on the shell with felt tip pens, then fill with compost or cotton wool. Dampen with water and sprinkle on cress seeds. Do not allow the seeds to dry out, sprinkling them with a few drops of water when necessary, and you will have a crop of cress for your sandwiches in a matter of a few days!

Felt egg cosies

Why not stick with tradition and have boiled eggs for breakfast, keeping them warm with colourful felt egg cosies.

You will need:
coloured felt
needle and thread
scissors
pins

1 Cut two basic cover shapes from felt – a sort of semicircular shape. Cut further shapes from felt scraps, to decorate. Choose from flowers, chicks, a bright red heart – whatever you like!

2 Stitch the shapes to one side of the cover. Stitch the two covers together, sandwiching an arch shape with a zigzag edge, cut from a contrasting coloured felt.

Flags and Frills

When you're having a party, decorate the house to put everyone in celebratory mood! All you need is coloured paper, scissors, string and glue!

Mexican fiesta flags

At fiesta time, the streets of Mexico are hung with strings of brightly coloured tissue paper flags. Make your own to hang in the house or garden.

You will need:
tissue paper
scissors
string
sticky tape or glue stick

1 Cut tissue paper into rectangles, approximately 20cm x 15cm.

2 Fold each one in half, then in half again and make lots of little cuts, then open out the paper. Make lots of flags, in a different colours. If you have scissors with zigzag blades, use these to trim the edges, or use a paper punch to make circular holes.

3 Fold the top edge of the flag over a length of string and glue or tape in place.

Party bunting

Cut triangle shapes from pieces of coloured paper and fold the top edge over a length of string.

Paper cake frill

Measure the circumference of your cake and add 2cm for overlap. Cut two or three strips of coloured tissue paper this length and about 9cm wide. Cut a strip of patterned paper this length and about 5cm wide. Stick the paper strips together along the centre, using a glue stick. Then use scissors to snip a frill along both edges of the tissue. Wrap the cake frill around your cake and glue the ends together.

Trick or Treat

It has become part of the Halloween tradition to dress up and visit neighbours' houses where, if you are lucky, you may get a treat. Here are some quick dressing-up ideas and a bucket to make, in which to collect your booty!

Collection bucket

Cover a giant waxed paper cup – the kind you get from the cinema, with popcorn or soft drinks – with papier mâché to strengthen it and give a good surface for painting.

You will need:
large paper cup
newspaper
PVA glue
paints
paintbrushes
glitter or glitter glue

1 Brush the cup, inside and out, with diluted PVA glue and cover with two or three layers of papier mâché. Leave to dry.

2 Paint the outside black and the inside in a contrasting colour.

3 When the paint is dry, decorate with a spider's web, using a glitter glue stick or PVA painted on and sprinkled with glitter.

Invitations

Cut a pumpkin head shape from orange paper, stick to yellow paper and cut out again, leaving a small margin of yellow all round the orange shape. Make lots of these and stick to rectangles of card, to make Halloween invitations, adding stick-on letters to spell out the word 'party'.

You can also make place cards for the table by sticking the paper cutouts onto pieces of folded card.

Halloween cards

Send a friend a spooky greeting with a paper cutout card. For a really simple design, cut a skull and crossbones from white paper and stick on to a folded sheet of black A4 card. For something a bit more intricate, cut the outline of a spooky landscape, complete with haunted castle, from black paper and stick on to folded orange card. Cut a white paper moon and little ghosts, and black bats.

Devilish horns

Tape horn shapes, cut from cardboard, on to a plastic hair band. Cover this with three layers of papier mâché, to make it sturdy and to give a good surface for painting. When dry, paint the band black and the horns red and you are all set to be a little devil!

Countdown to Christmas

Counting the days to Christmas? Here's a special clock to make, to help you keep track of the time, and notepads for jotting down Christmas wish lists.

Advent clock

The clock face has numbers from one to 24, so you can count down to Christmas Day, and award yourself – or someone else – a little present each time you move the pointer!

1 Cut a hexagon shape from cardboard and six squares, the same measurements as each side of the hexagon. Tape one square to each side of the hexagon, then tape edges of squares together, so you have a box. Stand this box on one of its sides and cut pieces of card to construct boxes on either side, using the clock in the picture as a guide.

You will need:
thick cardboard
PVA glue
newspapers
paints
paintbrushes
paper fastener
felt tip pen

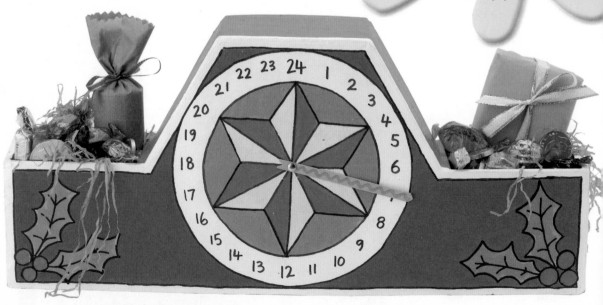

2 Brush the construction with diluted PVA glue and cover with torn newspaper strips, building up two or three layers and paying particular attention to edges and joins. Leave to dry.

3 Paint the clock face with a star and the side boxes with Christmas motifs, such as holly.

4 Cut a strip of card and make a hole in one end. Make a hole in the centre of the clock face. Use a paper fastener to attach the card strip to the clock face. Write the numbers on the clock face using a felt tip pen.

Nifty Christmas notepads

Cut a snowman shape from cardboard. Make the body large enough to stick on a pad of sticky notes and you have somewhere to write all your Christmas lists! Why not make several nifty notepads – a Christmas tree, perhaps, an angel, or a carol singer – and give them away as Christmas presents!

87

Cards and Wrap

Home-made cards are much more special than ones from a shop, and cheaper too. And while you are at it, why not make your own wrapping paper and gift tags?

Sparkly tree cards

You can create a three-dimensional effect by cutting the tree shapes from thick cardboard.

1 Cut triangle shapes for trees. Cover each one by sticking on felt, or pipe cleaners cut into strips, or coloured paper.

2 Fold sheets of card in half and decorate the front of each with a rectangle of coloured or metallic paper. Stick tree shapes in place.

You will need:
A5 sheets of coloured card
scrap cardboard
scraps of coloured, corrugated and metallic paper
glitter glue, sequins, felt, pipe cleaners and other trimmings
glue stick

3 Cut bucket shapes from corrugated paper and stick in place.

4 Now you can have great fun decorating the trees, using glitter glue, beads and sequins.

Christmas star cards

Fold coloured card in half. Square cards work best with star shapes. Cut stars from coloured or textured paper and decorate with glitter glue and sequins.

Printed giftwrap

Rubber stamps are easy to use and there is a very wide choice available. Or you could cut a shape from a potato and use that instead. Buy plain coloured wrapping paper, or brown parcel paper, lay it flat on a table, and print your design all over.

While you have the rubber stamps out, use them to make cards and gift tags. Tear paper into squares and rectangles and print with stamps, then stick onto coloured card, adding lengths of string for tying to parcels.

Deck the Halls

On Christmas Eve, make sure you have a stocking ready to hang up! And while you are waiting for Santa to call, keep yourself busy making paper chains to decorate the house!

Christmas stocking

Make your Christmas stocking any size you like and decorate it with your initial so Santa will know whose it is! Fleece fabric is relatively inexpensive and easy to sew because it does not fray. If you don't fancy stitching on the decorations, stick them in place with fabric glue.

You will need:
paper template
pins
scissors
red fleece fabric
coloured felt
needle and thread
fabric glue (optional)
sequins
glitter glue
ribbon

2 Choose which side is to be the front, and cut out shapes from felt, to decorate it. Cut out your initial, a wiggly strip to decorate the top, and some squares to represent presents. Stick or stitch all the felt shapes in place.

3 Add a touch of sparkle by stitching or gluing on sequins.

4 With wrong sides together, stitch all round the stocking, leaving the top edge open. The seam will be on the outside of the finished stocking. Add a loop of ribbon, for hanging, if you wish.

1 Cut two stocking shapes from fleece. This is easiest to do if you first make a a paper template and pin it to a double layer of fabric.

Paper chains

This traditional decoration remains popular because it is so easy to make. You can buy coloured paper strips in shops but why not cut your own, then you can make your chains any size you like.

You will need:
coloured paper
scissors
glue stick

1 Cut paper into equal sized strips. For a large chain, 21cm x 2cm is about right, or for a small chain, 11cm x 1cm. These measurements allow for 1cm overlap.

2 Apply glue to one end of a strip and attach to the other end, creating a ring. For the next and each subsequent strip, first push the strip through the previous loop you have made, before sticking the ends together. In this way, each strip becomes linked to the next, creating a chain.

3 Make the chain as long as you like, and suspend it across a ceiling or drape it over the branches of your Christmas tree.

Mini Christmas stockings

Little stockings, made from felt, are just the thing for hanging on the tree, or giving to someone, with a little gift inside.

Jazz Up Your Room

Introduction

When it comes to decorating your bedroom, you may or may not have a choice in the colour of the walls and carpet, or in the furniture, but there are things you can do to personalize your space.

Interior designers are not just concerned with big things like walls and floors – when designing a room, they know it's the details that make the difference!

In *Jazz Up Your Room*, some of the ideas are quick and easy to achieve, for an almost instant transformation, while others will take a bit more time but will be worth it in the end.

Are you bored with your colour scheme, want to add a few splashes of colour or touches of glitter and magic? Or are you simply stuck for space, with nowhere to put all your bits and pieces?

Crafty tips

When buying fabric dye, ask a shop assistant for advice. You will need cold water dyes that are suitable for cotton fabrics and are permanent (so they won't wash out). You will probably need to use a special dye fixative and some salt, too. Be sure to check the instructions on the pack of dye before you start.

Do you need some ideas? What about a money box for your loose change; somewhere to store your magazines; containers for pencils, CDs, tissues and other clutter; and a way of displaying photographs? Or a mobile, or perhaps you would rather make a cosy bed cover and some soft cushions to add a bit of comfort?

WARNING: It's your space, but...

It is wonderful to have the chance to express yourself creatively – but don't get carried away!

You will need to ask someone's permission before you start making any changes. And even if you have been given the go-ahead, always ask the advice of a grown-up before decorating walls, windows, floors and doors because if you use the wrong paint or glue, for example, you could do irreparable damage!

Fortunately, the ideas in *Jazz Up Your Room* are all pretty safe and do not involve a total room makeover! The ideas in these pages are just accessories to add personalized finishing touches!

Still, grown-up help could be useful with some of the trickier techniques, such as knitting, stitching, printing and dyeing!

94

Materials

For all the painted projects pictured in these pages, acrylic paints have been used. Acrylics come in a wide range of colours. Some have a matt finish, while some dry to a sheen, and you can even buy a range of metallic colours, including gold, bronze and silver, which will give a papier mâché vase or picture frame a really smart finish.

Fabric paints are also useful for quick transformations. These come in pots and can be painted on to fabric with a brush, or printed, using stamps. You may also like to try dyeing fabrics such as sheets, pillowcases and curtains. Ask your local craft shop for advice in buying the right type of dye. Tubes of glossy, pearly, glittery and metallic fabric paints are also useful, not only for fabric but for squiggling over frames and papier mâché models, and for sticking on fake jewels for a really glitzy effect.

Getting started

If you are making something from papier mâché, bear in mind that it takes time, not only to make the item, but to allow for glue and paint to dry. The projects described here use PVA glue, diluted with water, and strips of newspaper, built up on a base. If the base is constructed from cardboard, you will need to build up about three (or preferably four) layers of glue and paper. If the base is a balloon or mould which will be removed when the papier mâché is dry, aim for seven or eight (or even ten) layers, for a really sturdy and long-lasting result. And the bigger your model, the more PVA and newspaper you will need – so be prepared!

Sewing and knitting, too, even if they are quite straightforward, may take more time and effort than you think – but the more effort you put into a project, the better the end result! That's the theory, anyway.

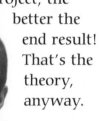

Making an Entrance

Make a sign for your bedroom
door and a bunch of paper
flowers to add a splash of colour!

Paper flowers

Because crêpe paper can be stretched, it is ideal
for making paper flowers as the petals can be pulled
into shape. Display the finished blooms in a vase, or fix
them around the edge of a mirror. The instructions
given will make ten flowers.

You will need:
crêpe paper, 50cm wide, in
green, pink, yellow and orange
lengths of wire
sticky tape or
double-sided tape

1 Cut lengths of
pink, orange
and yellow
crêpe paper measuring
60cm. Cut each strip
lengthways into 5 strips,
so each measures
60cm x 10cm.

2 Fold the pink and orange strips
in half, four times, then cut the
top third of each folded piece
into a v-shape, using plain or zigzag
scissors. Cut slits between the petals,
cutting down a further third of the
width of the strip. Open out.

3 Cut each yellow strip in half, so each
measures 30cm x 10cm. Snip each strip
into a fringe, stretch slightly and roll up
around one end of a piece of wire. Fasten in place
with sticky tape. This makes the flower centre.

4 Now roll a prepared pink or orange paper strip around the flower centre, pleating the uncut edge as you go. Tape in place.

5 Cut the green paper into twenty 2.5cm wide strips. Using two strips for each flower, wind the paper around the base of the flower and round the wire stem, stretching it slightly as you go.

6 To finish each flower, stretch the paper petals slightly, pulling them into shape with your fingertips – but take care not to tear the paper!

Door knob hanger

To make the shape, draw a circle with a smaller circle inside, then a long, narrow rectangle joined on. Cut out the shape from coloured thin card, cutting a gap in the ring so it can be slipped over your door handle. Stick two different coloured shapes back to back for a reversible hanger, and put a different message on each side. You could write 'do not disturb' or, better still, stick on a scary photo of yourself to frighten everyone away. Or write a welcoming greeting, or stick on a smiley face if you want to encourage visitors!

Grrrr!

Star signs

Cut out a five-pointed star from card, then cut out a picture of yourself and stick it in the centre. Punch a hole in the top point of the star and tie on a length of ribbon, to hang it up.

Warning bells

Thread small bells on to a length of wire and twist the ends to form a circle. Tie on larger bells using lengths of ribbon and tie on a ribbon loop for hanging. Hang it on your bedroom door and the bells will jingle and tinkle every time someone opens the door!

Storage Solutions

Keep your room tidy with these storage ideas – they're easy to make and you could decorate them to co-ordinate with your room scheme!

You will need:
thick card, from a cardboard box
ruler
pencil
sticky tape
gummed brown parcel tape
paint
paintbrush

CD box

This box will hold ten standard compact discs and you can decorate it in any way you like. It is made from card and is easily assembled using gummed brown parcel tape, available from stationers and art shops.

1 Measure and cut pieces of thick card. You will need a piece 14cm x 12.5cm for the base, 12.5cm x 7.5cm for the front, and 16cm x 12.5cm for the back. For the sides, cut two rectangles, 16cm x 14cm, then cut these to shape by marking a point 7.5cm along one long side and drawing a curved line from this point to the opposite top corner.

2 Assemble the box, using the finished box, pictured here, as a guide, and sticking pieces together with sticky tape.

3 Cover the whole box, paying particular attention to the corners and edges, with brown parcel tape, moistened with water. Leave to dry for about 1 hour.

4 Now decorate your box. Paint it in your choice of colours, then paint designs, or stick on paper cutouts, using diluted PVA glue.

Dustbin

You don't have to throw your rubbish
in this bin – why not keep treasures in
it instead?

You will need:
corrugated cardboard
sticky tape
PVA glue
paintbrush
newspapers
acrylic paints

1 Cut a rectangle of
corrugated card measuring
70cm x 25cm and roll it into a
cylinder. Tape the two short sides together.

2 Stand the cylinder on a piece of cardboard
and draw round it, to make a circular base.
Cut out the base and tape it in place.

3 To make the lid, cut a strip of corrugated
cardboard about 3cm wide and long enough
to go around the bin with a small overlap –
about 75cm in total. Cut a circle for the top of
the lid and tape it to the rim. Cut a strip of card
to make a handle, bend it and tape it in place.

4 Pour some PVA glue into a plastic
pot or jam jar and mix it with an
equal amount of water. Brush the
mixture all over the dustbin and lid,
inside and out, then apply pieces of
newspaper, torn into strips. Build up
about four layers of paper and glue in
this way, and leave to dry.

5 Paint the finished bin with a
layer of white paint, leave this
to dry, then paint it light grey
all over. Mix up several darker shades
of grey to paint in the details.

Home Sweet Home

Add a few homely touches to your room with these fun objects. They are enjoyable to make and each one has a practical use!

House tissue box

Disguise a square box of tissues as a little house and pull tissues out of the 'smoking' chimney! Simply measure your box of tissues and cut walls and roof pieces from thick card, slightly larger than the box, so it will fit inside. Assemble the house by sticking the walls and roof together with sticky tape. Don't forget to cut a hole in the roof and make a chimney, too. Then cover your model with four layers of papier mâché. Pour some PVA glue into a plastic pot or jam jar and mix it with an equal amount of water. Brush the mixture all over, then apply pieces of newspaper, torn into strips. Build up about four layers of paper and glue in this way, and leave to dry. Paint the house using acrylic paints.

House money box

Make this in exactly the same way as the tissue box but add a flat base and cut a slot in the roof. Keep putting money in the slot and your savings will be as safe as houses! When the house is full of money, you can get it out by cutting a hole in the base.

Chair money box

Easily assembled from offcuts of card, you can paint this chair to match your room and even make some little cushions for it, from scraps of fabric.

1 Cut an 18cm square of card, for the base. Cut a rectangle measuring 18cm x 12cm for the seat and three rectangles 18cm x 9cm for the front and sides. Tape all these in place.

2 For the back, cut a rectangle 20cm x 18cm and tape this in place. Cut another rectangle 18cm x 11cm and tape this to the back of the seat. These pieces form the chair back; round off the two top corners of each piece.

3 Cut a strip of corrugated cardboard 6cm wide and long enough to go over the top of the chair back – about 45cm – and tape this in place. Cut a slot in the centre.

4 For the chair arms, cut two 12cm squares of corrugated card, roll them up and tape in position.

5 Brush the whole structure with diluted PVA glue and apply torn newspaper. Build up at least four layers. Leave to dry.

5 Paint the chair white, to cover up the newsprint, then paint it in your choice of colour. To paint daisies, first print the flowers centres by dipping the flat end of a pencil in yellow paint and stamping spots all over the chair. Add white petals by dipping a soft paintbrush in paint and laying the brush fairly flat, to make a petal-shaped impression.

101

On the Shelf

A clock and bookends will add a touch of class to your room. The clock really works and the bookends can be made to represent any letters of the alphabet!

Cardboard clock

This elegant clock is simply constructed out of cardboard. Buy the battery-operated clock works from a craft supplier.

You will need:
thick cardboard
round cardboard or plastic lid
scissors
plastic bag
sand or pebbles
corrugated cardboard
PVA glue
sticky tape
2 paper pulp balls
newspapers
acrylic paints
paintbrush
sponge
battery-operated
clock works

1 For the base, construct a box from card, with the top and base measuring 20cm x 8cm, and the sides 5cm high. Fill a plastic bag with sand or pebbles, seal it and place inside the box, to give the finished clock some weight and to prevent it from toppling over.

2 For the front of the clock, cut a rectangle of cardboard 36cm x 22cm. Place the battery pack for the clock works in the centre of the card, draw around it and cut this shape out. Draw a line across, 9cm down from the top edge of the card, then draw a circle in the centre with a radius of about 6cm, using the clock on this page as a guide. Cut out the shape at the top. Draw around this shape on to a piece of card 20cm x 9cm; this piece will go at the back. For the sides, cut strips of card 27cm x 3.5cm. Tape these side pieces to the weighted box then tape the front of the clock in place and the back piece.

3 Cut a strip of corrugated cardboard 3.5cm wide and long enough to go across the top of the clock, fitting around the curved shape – about 26cm. Then tape on two small triangles at the top back corners, to help make the structure really strong.

4 For the columns at the sides, cut two 28cm squares of corrugated card and roll them up tightly. Tape in place and top with paper pulp balls. For the clock face, use a round cardboard or plastic lid glued in place. Make a hole in the centre, through both lid and cardboard, so you can insert the clock works later.

5 Dilute PVA glue with an equal amount of water and brush the mixture all over the clock, then apply pieces of newspaper, torn into strips. Build up about four layers of paper and glue in this way, and leave to dry.

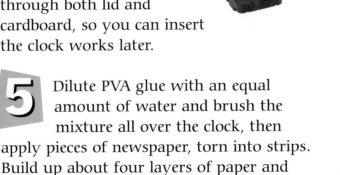

6 Paint the finished clock white, then dab on pale blue paint with a sponge. Cut out numbers and stick them on, or paint them directly on to the clock face.

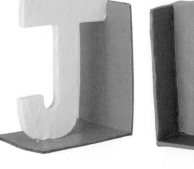

103

7 Fit the clock works, which should fit snugly into the hole you have cut.

Alphabet bookends

Cut your chosen letter from thick cardboard. Make it about 20cm high. You will need two or three shapes exactly the same. Glue them together to make a thick letter shape.

Then cut the base, 17cm x 12cm and back piece, 19cm x 12cm. Join these together, then tape the letter in place. Cover the structure with four layers of papier mâché (see step 5 of the clock), leave to dry, then paint in your choice of bright colours.

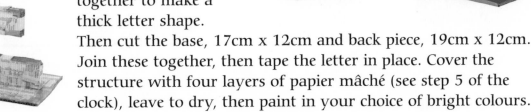

Cushions

These cushions will add colour and comfort to your room and are a great way to express your creativity!

Painted cushion

Recycle an old sheet or pillowcase to make this colourful cushion. If you are using new fabric, wash and dry it before you start painting.

You will need:
white cotton fabric, 40cm square
newspaper
fabric paints
paintbrush
cork
needle and thread
red cotton fabric, 37cm square
35cm square cushion pad

1 Lay the white fabric flat, on plenty of newspaper. Paint dark red stripes, 6cm apart. Then paint orange stripes. By the time you have done these, the dark red ones should be dry and you can paint bright red stripes, then yellow ones.

2 Pour a little blue paint on to a saucer or plastic lid, dip a cork into the paint and use it to print large dots in the spaces between the stripes you have painted.

3 Leave to dry completely, then press with a hot iron (you may need an adult's help with this), according to the instructions on the pots of fabric paint. This will fix the colour into the fabric and make it permanent.

4 Trim the edges of the painted fabric so you are left with a square measuring 37cm. Place it on top of the red fabric square, painted side facing inwards, and stitch round three sides, 1cm from the edges. Turn right sides out, insert the cushion pad, tuck in the raw edges and sew the opening closed.

Crafty tips

Make your own cushion pad from scrap fabric, filling it with polyester toy stuffing. The advantage of using a cushion pad is that you can remove your cover when it is dirty, and wash it.

Patchwork cushion cover

You don't have to be an expert at sewing to stitch a cushion – it's really easy! You just have to be able to stitch two pieces of fabric together in a straight line, by hand or using a sewing machine if you have access to one.

You will need:
scraps of cotton fabrics
needle and thread
40cm x 30cm cushion pad

Heart cushion

Use soft, fluffy fleece to make this cover. Cut a heart shaped template from paper and use this as a pattern to cut out two heart shaped pieces of fleece. Stitch them together, 1cm from the edges, leaving a small opening. Turn right sides out, stuff with polyester toy filling and sew the opening closed.

1 Cut six 12cm squares of fabric, all different. Try to combine your own selection of plain, striped and printed designs. Stitch three squares together to form a strip, with 1cm seams, stitch another strip of three squares then stitch the two strips together.

2 Now cut a rectangle of fabric 32cm x 14cm and stitch it to one side of the piece you have made. Cut another piece, 32cm x 9cm and join this on, too. You should now have a piece measuring 42cm x 32cm. Cut a plain piece of fabric this size, for the back of the cover, place it on top of the patchwork, right side facing inwards, and stitch round three sides, 1cm from the edges.

3 Turn right sides out, insert the cushion pad, tuck in the raw edges and sew the opening closed.

Bed Time

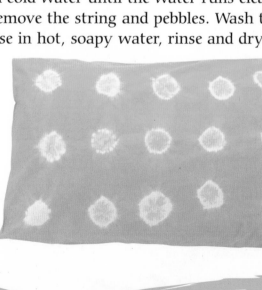

Instead of plain pillows, why not have patterned ones? Decorate them yourself, using fabric paint or dye.

Tie-dye pillowcase

Start with a plain, pale coloured pillowcase and a tin of cold water dye, suitable for cotton fabrics.

You will need:
cotton pillowcase
cold water dye
small pebbles
string
rubber gloves
plastic bucket

1 Wash the pillowcase, wring out most of the water but leave it damp.

2 Tie pebbles into the fabric, tying tightly with short lengths of string.

3 Make up the dye powder according to the packet instructions and put it in the plastic bucket. Protecting your hands with rubber gloves, immerse the pillowcase in the dye and leave it for the recommended length of time – about 1 hour.

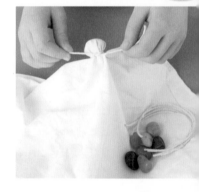

4 Remove the pillowcase from the dye and rinse in cold water until the water runs clear, then remove the string and pebbles. Wash the pillowcase in hot, soapy water, rinse and dry.

Printed pillowcase

Use fabric paint to decorate a pillowcase. The one in the picture was printed with rubber-stamped stars and a moon shape cut from a potato.

1 Lay the pillowcase flat on a surface protected with plenty of newspaper. Place a thick wad of newspaper inside the pillowcase so the paint doesn't soak through to the back.

2 Slice the potato in half and cut out a moon shape from one half. You may need the help of an adult to do this.

3 Brush the surface of the potato with fabric paint and press it into position on the pillowcase. Repeat to make lots of printed moon shapes.

4 Stamp stars using a different colour. You can cut your own star shape from the other half of the potato, or use a rubber stamp if you have one.

107

5 Leave to dry completely, then press with a hot iron, (you may need an adult's help) according to the instructions on the pots of fabric paint. This will fix the colour into the fabric and make it permanent.

Pyjama bag

Make a simple bag from two pieces of striped fabric, 45cm x 35cm, stitched together round three sides. Cut two pieces of spotty fabric 45cm x 14cm, fold and stitch to the top of the bag and thread with cord, to make drawstrings. Neaten the ends with fabric scraps.

Very Cosy

A cosy patchwork blanket requires the most basic of knitting skills, while a woolly snake draught excluder can be made from old clothes!

Patchwork blanket

Collect balls of double knitting wool in a variety of colours. You could use all the colours of the rainbow, or stick to shades of your favourite colours – such as purples, pinks and greens! One 50g ball of yarn will make three or four squares, depending on how tightly or loosely you knit!

You will need:
4.5mm knitting needles
double knitting wool
tapestry needle

Crafty tip
To make 42 squares, you will need approximately 600g of wool – that's twelve 50g balls!

1 Cast on 25 stitches and knit 45 rows. You should have a square of knitting. If your knitting is not square, you may have to knit a few more rows (or a few less!).

2 Keep knitting until you have a whole pile of squares. Each time you finish a square, break off the yarn leaving a piece about 25cm long. These long ends will be threaded into your tapestry needle and used to sew the squares together.

3 The blanket pictured is made from 42 squares. Stitch six squares together in a row. Repeat until you have seven strips, each made of six squares, then join the strips together.

Snake draught excluder

If the wind whistles under your bedroom door or window, this is just what you need. Or you may just want it as a mascot or another cuddly toy! To make a snake, simply cut the foot off a long sock or the sleeve off an old jumper. Make the front end of the snake by stitching 1cm from the cut edge and pulling the thread to gather the fabric. Tuck the raw edges inside and stitch a tongue in place, cut from red felt. Stuff the tube with polyester toy stuffing, then stitch the edges of the cuff together neatly. Finally, stitch on eyes cut from black and white felt.

Cosy hat

You could use wool left over from your blanket to make a stylish hat! Using 4mm knitting needles, cast on 160 stitches. Knit about 70 rows in stripes of different colours. Cast off, then fold the knitting in half and stitch the two short sides together. Stitch across the top.

Add a couple of knitted strips and tie them together, then roll up the edge to make a brim.

Going Wild!

Accessories decorated with animal prints can make your room look wildly glamorous – or just wild!

Tiger bowl

Make a papier mâché shell and add a base, then decorate it with tiger stripes or your own favourite animal print.

1 Blow up the balloon to the size you want your finished bowl to be and stand the knotted end in a jam jar, taping it in place.

2 Dilute PVA glue with water and brush it over three-quarters of the balloon. Cover with torn newspaper strips. Build up at least eight layers of papier mâché in this way. For a really strong result, aim for ten layers. When dry, burst the balloon, leaving a thick papier mâché shell.

3 Trim the edge, so you have a bowl shape. Turn it upside down and glue the cardboard tube in place. Add a strip of corrugated cardboard, rolled around the end of the tube, to make a base.

4 Cover the base and the trimmed edge of the bowl with three more layers of papier mâché. Leave to dry.

5 Paint the bowl, inside and out, with white paint, to cover the newsprint and give a good base for painting. Then paint it two shades of yellowy-orange. Leave to dry and paint on black stripes. Paint the inside in a colour of your choice.

110

You will need:
round balloon
PVA glue
newspapers
cardboard tubes from toilet roll
corrugated cardboard
paintbrush
acrylic paints

Giraffe frame
To make the frame, glue a small square box or box lid inside a slightly larger one and cover the gap between the two with card strips, to create a frame. Paint the edge of the frame with a giraffe pattern. Paint the background and the inside of the frame with a scene including a painted giraffe, then place plastic giraffes in the frame for a 3D effect.

Leopard vase

This is also made from papier mâché but this time the shape is moulded round a long balloon!

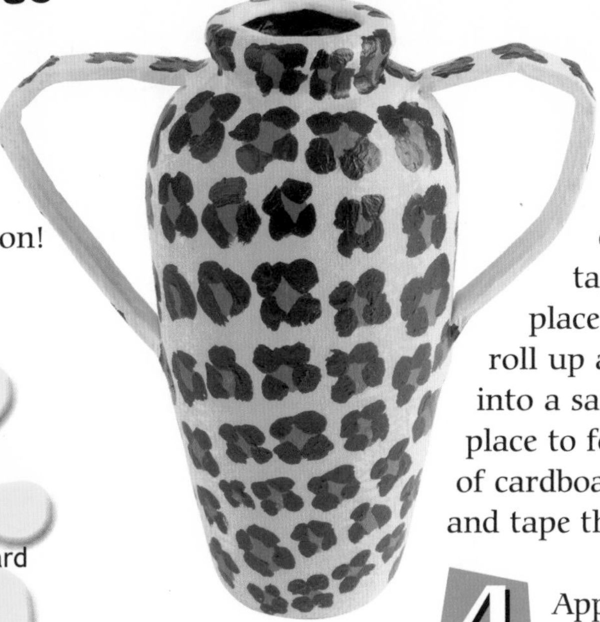

You will need:
1 long balloon
newspapers
PVA glue
corrugated cardboard
sticky tape
paints and brushes

1 Blow up the balloon to the size you want your finished vase to be.

2 Follow step 2 of the method for making the Tiger bowl.

3 Trim both ends of the papier mâché shell. Decide which will be the base and cut a circle of card to fit, taping it securely in place. On the neck end, roll up a sheet of newspaper into a sausage and tape this in place to form a rim. Cut strips of cardboard to make handles and tape these in place, too.

4 Apply three more layers of papier mâché to the base, handles and rim. Leave to dry.

5 Paint the vase, first with a base coat of white, then with two shades of yellowy-orange. Dab with spots of brown, then outline these spots with dabs of black paint, using the vase pictured here as a guide.

Magazine boxes

Recycle cereal, washing powder or cat food boxes by covering them with wrapping paper and you'll have somewhere to store all your magazines, booklets or catalogues! Cut off the top flaps, then cut diagonally across the front and back of the box. Place the box on a sheet of wrapping paper and draw each side, adding a margin of about 1.5cm. Stick the paper to the box, using a glue stick – or use self-adhesive paper – and tuck the excess paper inside the box. Make a set of boxes in different sizes and line them up on a shelf. You could label each box with its contents.

Hanging Around

T he projects on this page should be suspended from the ceiling, window frame or doorway, or from below a shelf, for maximum impact!

Dream catcher

Hang this above your bed to filter out all the bad dreams and let only the good ones through!

You will need:
wooden ring from embroidery frame
cotton yarn
wooden beads
feathers

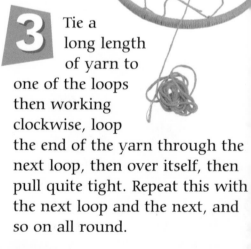

1 Start by binding the whole ring with yarn. Cut a long length of yarn, knot one end around the ring and wind the yarn round and round. You may have to use more than one piece of yarn, knotting the ends to the ring to fasten them off.

2 Now make loops with the yarn, all the way round, knotting the yarn firmly to the ring as you go.

3 Tie a long length of yarn to one of the loops then working clockwise, loop the end of the yarn through the next loop, then over itself, then pull quite tight. Repeat this with the next loop and the next, and so on all round.

4 When you have threaded the yarn through every loop, start on the next row, doing exactly the same, and continuing in a spiral until you are near the centre of the ring.

5 Thread a few beads on to the yarn and proceed as before until you reach the centre, then knot off the yarn.

6 Do not cut the end of the yarn yet but thread a few beads on to it and tie a feather to the end. The beads should slip over the feather quite easily.

7 Add further lengths of yarn, knotted to the ring, threaded with beads and with feathers on the end. Then add a loop of yarn to the opposite side of the ring, for hanging.

Bead curtain

Choose a length of wooden doweling the width you want your curtain to be. To it, tie lengths of strong cotton yarn, about 2cm apart, and about one and a half times the length you want your finished curtain to be. Thread beads on to each string, making knots in between to create spaces between the beads. Use glass or plastic beads, or even plastic drinking straws cut into short lengths. Hang your finished curtain from two hooks, placed either side of your window or doorway.

113

Sun and moon mobile

Use a round lid from a plastic tub, as a base. Then roll up or crumple small pieces of tissue paper or kitchen paper, dip them in diluted PVA glue, and use them to mould features. On one side, make a sun face, with a circular rim, nose, cheeks and eyebrows.

On the other side, mould the shape of a new moon, again with nose, mouth and other features. Leave to dry, then paint with acrylics. Add a length of ribbon for hanging.

Dressing Up

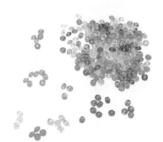

Introduction

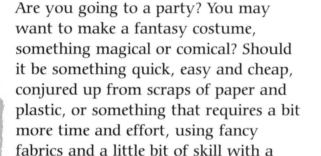

Dressing Up is about everyday style as well as fancy dress for those special occasions! Make some jewellery, a hair band or a bag – or make a whole outfit, it's up to you! And it's such fun to wear something you have made yourself!

Are you going to a party? You may want to make a fantasy costume, something magical or comical? Should it be something quick, easy and cheap, conjured up from scraps of paper and plastic, or something that requires a bit more time and effort, using fancy fabrics and a little bit of skill with a needle and thread?

Or do you simply want to add to your day-to-day wardrobe? It may be that you want to jazz up an existing outfit, or make some eye-catching accessories. You could start with something easy, like a simple necklace or bracelet, or try something a bit more challenging like a hair slide, hat

or bag. Whatever you decide to do, you'll find that all the ideas in *Dressing Up* are fun and creative!

Sew simple

Even if your sewing skills are pretty basic, accessories such as hats and bags – or even whole outfits – are not that hard to make. The instructions given in the following pages are easy to follow and an adult should be able to show you the basic stitches needed.

Fabrics and other materials

You don't have to spend a fortune on fabrics. Check out your wardrobe first of all, for clothes you have grown out of. Perhaps you can recycle them? Shirts, sweatshirts, T-shirts, jeans and even underwear and tights can all be given a new lease of life!

Jumble sales and charity shops are a good source of materials. An old sparkly evening dress, perhaps, that can be cut up and made into a fairy tutu? Or some broken necklaces that can be taken apart, and the beads rethreaded?

Dyes and fabric paints

A plain T-shirt that you are bored with could be given a whole new lease of life with some dye or a painted design. Craft shops are the place to go to find a selection of dyes. Don't be afraid to ask an assistant for advice if you are not sure which kind to buy. And get the help or permission of an adult before embarking on any messy activities like dyeing. Fabric paints are great fun to use. There is the kind sold in pots, for painting or printing, and those sold in tubes, which can be pearly, puffy or glittery, and are useful for squiggly designs or for sticking sequins and jewels to fabrics and craft projects.

Be prepared

If you are keen on sewing or jewellery-making, you may already have a workbox with basic equipment such as scissors, needles and thread and a tape measure.

It's useful to have several pairs of scissors, one for cutting fabric and another for cutting paper etc (tie a different coloured ribbon around the handle of each pair to remind yourself which is which). Cutting paper can blunt scissor blades and you need sharp scissors to cut through most fabrics. But be sure to be very careful with them – never carry scissors around and always put them away safely out of the reach of younger children.

Keep pins and needles in matchboxes or plastic film canisters. You will need a few small, sharp needles for sewing fabric, a long, fine one with a small eye for threading tiny beads and a larger, thicker, blunter one for stringing larger beads on thicker thread or yarn.

Visit your local craft shop or bead shop for beads in all shapes and sizes, strong beading thread and fastenings for necklaces or brooches. While you

are there, you could also spend some of your pocket money on coloured felt, ribbons, safety pins, feathers, fake jewels and fabric flowers.

Fabric shops often sell remnants – small pieces of fabric, usually offered at a reduced price – so look out for scraps of interesting fabrics, including net, fleece and animal prints. And ask any adults you know who do sewing, to save leftover scraps for you.

And for every kind of craft activity – not only the ones on the following pages – it is always useful to have a stock of paper (plain and textured), paints (preferably acrylics), glue (PVA, fabric glue and glue stick), sticky tape, wire and string.

Playing Pirates

Ahoy there! Take an old jumper and pair of trousers, plus some pieces of fabric, and create a costume for sailing the high seas!

Pirate flag

This flag, known as the Jolly Roger, struck terror into sailors' hearts. No self-respecting pirate would be without his or her skull and crossbones!

118

You will need:
black cotton fabric
needle and black thread
pencil and paper
white cotton fabric
fabric glue
wooden stick

1 Cut a rectangle of black fabric measuring 40cm x 30cm. Turn under 1cm all round, to form a hem. Stitch.

2 Draw a skull and crossbones on paper. When you are satisfied with your design, cut it out and pin it to the white fabric. Cut out the shapes and glue them to the black fabric.

3 Fold over 2cm on one side of the flag, and stitch, to form a channel. Stitch across the top. Insert the stick.

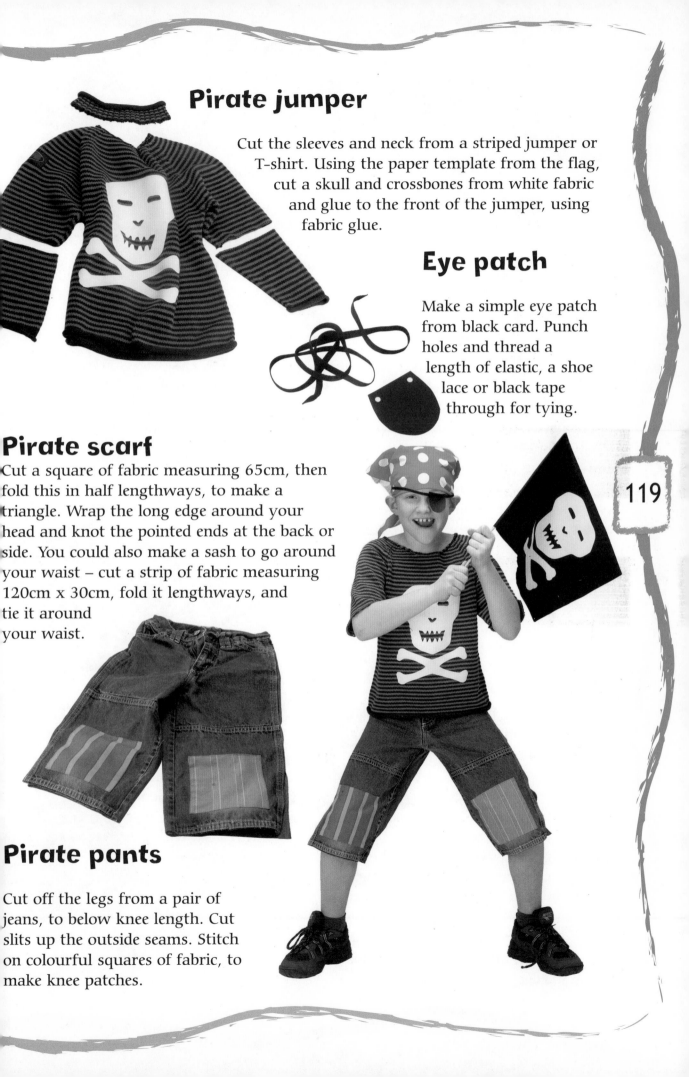

Pirate jumper

Cut the sleeves and neck from a striped jumper or T-shirt. Using the paper template from the flag, cut a skull and crossbones from white fabric and glue to the front of the jumper, using fabric glue.

Eye patch

Make a simple eye patch from black card. Punch holes and thread a length of elastic, a shoe lace or black tape through for tying.

Pirate scarf

Cut a square of fabric measuring 65cm, then fold this in half lengthways, to make a triangle. Wrap the long edge around your head and knot the pointed ends at the back or side. You could also make a sash to go around your waist – cut a strip of fabric measuring 120cm x 30cm, fold it lengthways, and tie it around your waist.

Pirate pants

Cut off the legs from a pair of jeans, to below knee length. Cut slits up the outside seams. Stitch on colourful squares of fabric, to make knee patches.

Hat Tricks

On a cold day, you'll want to wear a nice warm hat – particularly one you have made yourself! Try one of these – they are easy to make but sure to impress!

Heart hat

This hat is constructed from two squares of fleece fabric. When buying fleece, ask for a 30cm length, which should be enough to make two or three hats. Alternatively, cut up an old sweatshirt or tracksuit bottoms. Decorate your hat with a heart or your own choice of motif.

120

You will need:
two 29cm squares of purple fleece fabric
small scrap of red fleece
needle and thread

1 Lay the squares together and stitch up two opposite sides, about 1cm from edges.

2 Turn right sides out, so seams are on the inside, then flatten so that seams are in the centre.

3 Cut a heart shape from the red fleece and stitch on top of one of the seams.

4 Fold inside out again, and stitch along the top. Turn right sides out and fold the two top corners to the centre, securing them in place with a few firm stitches.

5 Fold over 2cm along the bottom edge, and stitch. Roll up this edge, to form a brim.

Snuggly scarf

For the simplest scarf, cut a rectangle of fabric measuring 120cm x 18cm. Snip a fringe at either end, with each strip about 12mm wide. Knot the end of each strip.

Tassel hat

Make this in exactly the same way as the heart hat but without the motif at the front. Do not stitch the top corners to the centre, but cut 14 strips of red fleece, 12cm x 1cm. Place six strips together and tie a strip around the centre, tightly, to make a tassel. Stitch the tassels to the two corners.

Pixie hat

This pointed hat is made by joining four pieces together. You could cut each section from a different coloured fleece!

You will need:
blue fleece fabric,
at least 65cm x 35cm
scrap of green
fleece fabric
paper and pencil
pins
needle and thread

1 Start by making a paper template. Draw a rectangle 15cm x 8cm. From the centre of one of the long sides, draw a line 23cm long. Join the end of this line to the two corners of the rectangle.

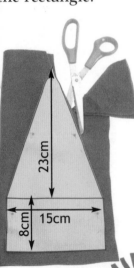

23cm
8cm
15cm

2 Pin the template to your fabric and cut out four fabric pieces.

3 Stitch the pieces together, to form a cone. Fold up 2cm along the bottom edge and stitch, to form a hem, then roll up to form a brim.

4 Make a tassel from three blue and three green strips and stitch to the top of the hat.

121

Fairy Fun

Most girls like to put on a pair of wings and wave a wand. It's easy to create your own little bit of fairy magic with these home-made fairy accessories.

Fairy skirt

Net is cheap to buy and available in a wide range of colours. This is easy to make but you may require some adult help with gathering the fabric.

You will need:
2m of 136cm wide net
1m of 7cm wide ribbon
needle and thread
elastic

1 Fold the net in half lengthways, then in half again, so you have four layers.

2 Stitch through the double fold of fabric, about 1cm from the fold, with a running stitch.

3 Pull up the thread, to gather the fabric, until the gathered edge measures 1m.

4 Fold the ribbon in half lengthways and place over the gathered edge. Pin in place, then stitch firmly through all layers, close to the edge of the ribbon.

5 Cut a piece of elastic long enough to go around your waist. Pin a safety-pin at the end of the elastic and use this to help thread it through the ribbon. Stitch the ends of the elastic and ribbon together. Cut through the folds on the bottom edge.

Fairy wand

Cut two star shape from thick cardboard and tape back to back, with the end of a stic in between. Paint the stars and the stick, adding glitter for sparkle and gluin on some jewels. Tie lengths of ribbon around the top of the stick.

Fairy wings

These require adult help, particularly when cutting and bending wire into shape. Use millinery wire or two coat hangers with the hooks cut off. Make sure you cover the sharp ends of the wire with plenty of tape. To join the two wings, any fabric will do but something shiny or metallic, such as silver lamé, looks best.

You will need:
1.8m medium gauge wire
pair of sheer tights
sticky tape
scraps of silver fabric
needle and thread
70cm narrow elastic
newspaper
pots of fabric paints
paintbrush
tubes of glittery and neon fabric paints

1 Cut the wire into two equal lengths and, using the wings pictured here as a guide, bend into wing shapes. Join the ends of the wire by binding them with sticky tape.

2 Cut the legs off a pair of tights and push one wing into each leg. Stitch the cut edges together at the point where the ends are joined.

3 Cut two pieces of fabric, each measuring 12cm x 8cm. Fold in the edges by about 1cm all round. Place one of the fabric pieces with the two short ends covering the joins in the wire and the cut edges of the tights. Stitch in place. Do the same with the other piece of fabric, on the other side of the wings.

4 Cut two 35cm lengths of elastic and stitch to the fabric, level with the inside edges of the wings, to form loops to slip over your shoulders.

5 Place the wings on a thick pile of newspaper and paint, using fabric paints, diluted with an equal amount of water. For the best effect, using two or three colours. Leave to dry – for about 2 hours.

6 Using glittery and neon fabric paints, squeeze squiggly patterns over the wings. Leave to dry, flat, overnight.

Customized T-shirts

Transform a plain white T-shirt into an explosion of colour and pattern with brilliant tie-dye.

Swirly T-shirt

This is a great way to smarten up an old T-shirt! If you are dyeing a new T-shirt, you will need to wash it first, or the dye may not soak into the fabric.

You will need:
cotton T-shirt
elastic bands
cold water dyes in blue,
red and yellow
rubber gloves
thick paintbrush

1 Wash your T-shirt, wring out most of the water but leave it damp.

2 For a swirly effect, lay the T-shirt flat, pinc the centre with your finger and thumb, and twist into a spiral. Secur the bundle with two elastic bands, dividing it into four sections.

3 Dissolve the dye powder in warm water, adding fixative and salt according to the packet instructions. Make up the three different colours separately.

4 Protect your work surface with plastic bags and your hands with rubber gloves. Use the paintbrush to apply dye to the T-shirt, painting each section a different colour. To achieve a similar effect to the T-shirt on this page, paint two opposite quarters blue, one yellow and one red. Make sure the fabric is well saturated with dye.

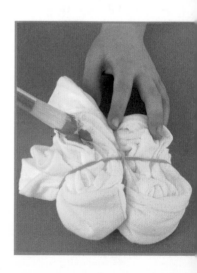

5 Place the T-shirt in a plastic bag, seal and leave overnight.

6 Remove the T-shirt from the bag and rinse in cold water until the water runs clear, then remove the elastic bands. Then wash the T-shirt in hot, soapy water, rinse and dry.

Crafty tips
• You could dye other items of clothing, too – cotton pants, socks or trousers, for example.
• When buying dyes, ask a shop assistant for advice. You will need cold water dyes that are suitable for cotton fabrics and are permanent (so they won't wash out). You will probably need to use a special dye fixative and some salt, too. Check the instructions in the pack of dye before you start.

Sunburst T-shirt

To achieve a sunburst or target effect, place the T-shirt on a flat surface, pinch the centre and lift. Add elastic bands at intervals, dividing the T-shirt into three or more sections, and dye each section a different colour.

Prehistoric Pranks

This is the easiest costume to make, as it requires no sewing, just a bit of artful arranging!

Caveman club

This primitive weapon looks heavy but is very lightweight – but it's just for decoration, so don't be tempted to hit anyone over the head with it!

You will need:
cardboard tube
empty plastic bottle
sticky tape
newspapers
PVA glue
paintbrush
acrylic paints

1 Place the cardboard tube over the neck of the bottle and tape firmly in place.

2 Roll up a sheet of newspaper, wrap it around the bottle and tape in place.

3 Pour some PVA glue into a plastic cup or a jam jar and add an equal amount of water. Stir well and brush the mixture all over the club, then apply pieces of newspaper, torn into strips. Build up about four layers of paper and glue in this way, and leave to dry.

4 Paint the finished club with a layer of white paint, leave to dry, then paint it brown.

Animal skin tunic

This costume is produced without any sewing – and its most sizes! From a piece of animal print fabric measuring 160cm x 85cm, cut a strip 10cm wide from one long side, to make a sash. Fold the remaining piece in half across its width and cut along the fold for 50cm. Place the fabric with the uncut 25cm on your shoulder, wrap the fabric around your body and tie the sash around your waist to hold it all in place.

Prehistoric hair

If you have short hair, dampen it slightly with water, then rub hair gel into it, particularly near the roots. Use your fingers to ruffle and spike the strands, making it look as spiky and tangled as possible. Tie a strip of fabric around your head. If you have long hair, tie it in a pony tail on top of your head. Wind a strip of fabric round and round the ponytail to make it stick up.

Ancient accessories

If you have any spare fabric, cut it into strips, about 5cm wide, and wrap these around your feet. You could wrap them around your wrists or upper arms, too, or use one to create a headband.

Bags of Ideas

Here are some bags that are stylish as well as practical and just require the most basic of sewing skills

Bear bag

Made from fleece and felt, which do not fray, this is easy to stitch.

You will need:
purple fleece fabric, at least
50cm x 20cm
coloured felt
needle and thread
60cm cord
button

1 Cut two pieces of fleece, each measuring 25cm x 20cm.

2 Cut the bear shape from brown felt and stitch in place on one of the pieces of fleece, using a contrasting coloured thread and running stitch.

3 Cut other details from felt and stitch in place, oversewing the edges neatly.

4 Place the two pieces of fleece together, with the bear motif inside. Stitch the sides and base together, 1cm from the edges. Turn under 2cm at the top edge, to form a hem and stitch in place.

5 Stitch the two ends of the cord to the side seams on the inside of the bag.

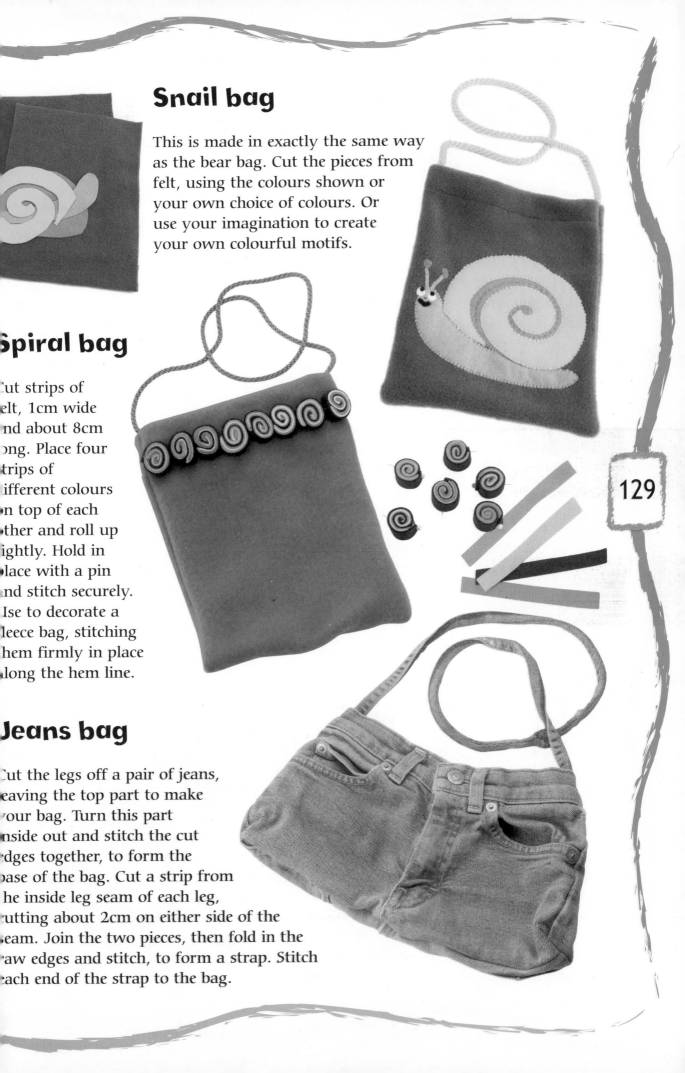

Snail bag

This is made in exactly the same way as the bear bag. Cut the pieces from felt, using the colours shown or your own choice of colours. Or use your imagination to create your own colourful motifs.

Spiral bag

Cut strips of felt, 1cm wide and about 8cm long. Place four strips of different colours on top of each other and roll up tightly. Hold in place with a pin and stitch securely. Use to decorate a fleece bag, stitching them firmly in place along the hem line.

Jeans bag

Cut the legs off a pair of jeans, leaving the top part to make your bag. Turn this part inside out and stitch the cut edges together, to form the base of the bag. Cut a strip from the inside leg seam of each leg, cutting about 2cm on either side of the seam. Join the two pieces, then fold in the raw edges and stitch, to form a strap. Stitch each end of the strap to the bag.

Desert Island Dreams

Even on a dull day, put on this costume and you will be transported to a tropical island. And all you need is some crêpe paper, tissue, fabric scraps and a few plastic bags!

Hula hula costume

Use your own choice of colours – crêpe paper is available in lots of bright colours – the brighter the better!

You will need:
crêpe paper, 50cm wide, in green, pink, yellow and orange
strip of fabric, 1.4m x 12cm
needle and thread

1 Cut two 60cm lengths of each colour of crêpe paper. This will be the length of the finished skirt.

2 Place the paper in two piles, each containing one sheet of each colour. Place the piles side by side, with one of the short edges uppermost.

3 Mark the centre point of the strip of fabric. Fold in the two long edges. Fold in half lengthways and place over the paper, to form a waistband. The centre point of the fabric should line up with the division between the two piles of paper. Stitch the waistband in place, through all thicknesses, so the paper is securely trapped inside the folded fabric.

4 Now cut the paper into strips, starting at the bottom edge and cutting towards the waistband.

Floral hair

Some artificial flowers, stitched to a hair slide, will help to dress up your hair.

Hula hula garland

Cut strips measuring 12cm wide from a plastic carrier bag and from coloured tissue paper. For a short garland, these strips should be about 80cm long and for a long garland, about 1m. Choose the most colourful, shiny plastic bag you can find and, if it's not big enough, you can cut several strips and join them together.

To make the garland, sandwich two or three strips of tissue paper between two strips of plastic. Stitch up the centre, through all layers, then join the two ends. Snip either side of the stitching, into a fringe, then crumple and ruffle the garland in your hands.

131

Fantastic Feathers

Native American head-dresses are the inspiration for this feathered headgear, which is colourful and as much fun to make as it is to wear.

Feather head-dress

You will really feel like a big chief when you wear this magnificent creation! It requires large and small feathers, available in craft shops. Red, yellow and green create an authentic effect but you could choose your own colour combination.

You will need:
red corrugated card
stapler
10 small green feathers
10 small red feathers
7 long feathers
10 small blue feathers
1 small yellow feather
28cm red marabou feather trim
37cm of 12mm elastic

1 Cut a circle with a diameter of 30cm from corrugated card. Cut this in half, then cut a 5cm strip from each half (and save these to make a head band).

2 Staple the green feathers, evenly spaced, to the inside of one of the card pieces, along the curved edge. Staple the red feathers in between.

3 Staple the long feathers, evenly spaced on top of the red and green ones.

4 Because the staples will now show at the front, staple the blue feathers to the front of the card, to hide them. Staple a yellow feather in the centre and staple the marabou trim along the bottom edge.

5 At the back of the card, staple the ends of the elastic to either side, then glue the second piece of card over the back, to hide the ends of the feathers and the staples.

Feather head band

Cut a strip of corrugated card 48cm long and 5cm wide (or join the two pieces you have left over from making the headdress). Join the two ends with two 10cm pieces of elastic, stapled to the card. Glue on paper cut-outs, then push feathers into the top of the band.

Hair braid

Cut three 90cm lengths of cotton yarn or embroidery thread, fold in half and tie a knot, to create a loop. Plait the strands and, when you get to the ends, thread on some beads and tie on a feather. The loop can be attached to a hair slide or an elastic band.

133

Beads and Pins

Thread small glass beads on elastic to make the simplest bracelets – and on to safety pins for a set of stylish jewellery. For something bolder, make your own beads from coloured paper!

Paper beads

For a different effect, or if you do not have sheets of coloured paper, use any scraps of paper you have available. You could use old letters or documents, for example, or pages cut from magazines.

You will need:
A4 sheets of coloured paper
knitting needle or stick
glue stick or
double-sided sticky tape

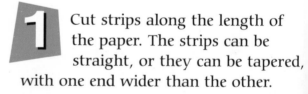

1 Cut strips along the length of the paper. The strips can be straight, or they can be tapered, with one end wider than the other.

2 Roll a strip around a knitting needle or stick, sticking the end down with a glue stick or double-sided tape.

3 Thread your home-made beads on to lengths of string, knotting the ends.

Friendship bracelets

Thread small glass or plastic beads on to narrow elastic. You can buy really thin, strong elastic specially designed for jewellery-making, from craft shops. Knot the ends of the elastic firmly, slipping the knot inside one of the beads.

Make bracelets from beads of all one colour and size, or mix colours and shapes, whichever you prefer.

Safety pin jewellery

Thread glass beads on to safety pins. To make a bracelet, thread one piece of cord elastic through the loops at one ends of the pins and another piece of elastic through the holes at the other ends of the pins. Add a bead in between each pin. Knot the ends of the elastic together.

To make a necklace, thread a length of string or cord through the pins, with beads in between.

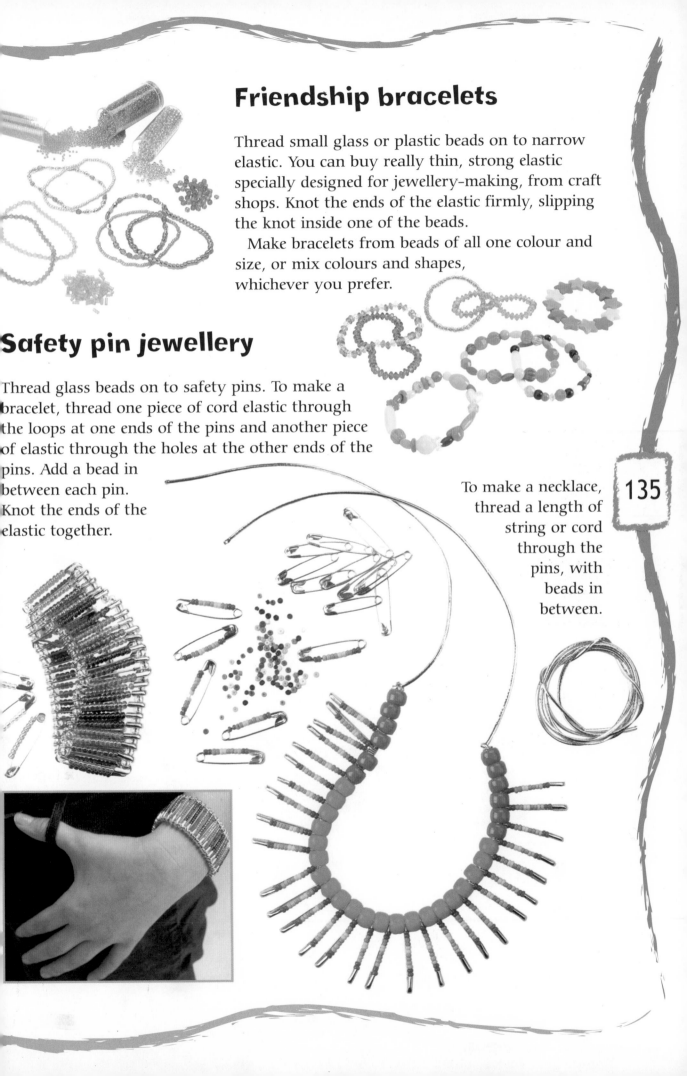

Outdoor Fun

Introduction

When the weather is fine, it is great to get outdoors and enjoy the sunshine. You may want to plant or you may want to play. Whatever you like doing, *Outdoor Fun* is packed with ideas to help you make the most of life in the garden!

If you are lucky enough to have access to a garden, you may be allowed your own space: perhaps a quiet corner where you can plant some flowers or herbs, or make a den? It may be, however, that your only outdoor space is a windowsill or balcony - but you can still test out your green fingers by planting something in a pot or trough and watching it grow!

And when you are out and about in the park or countryside, or by the sea, collect stuff like pebbles, shells, twigs and driftwood so that, on a rainy afternoon, you can turn them into something - a wind chime,

maybe, or a paperweight. Check out *Outdoor Fun* for some great projects using found objects.

Tools and materials

You may find what you need in the garden shed, or perhaps an adult can help you collect some stuff together. For planting projects, flower pots are useful, though you may be able to use other things as planting containers: baskets lined with plastic, yoghurt tubs, an old plastic bucket? Compost, gravel and broken clay pots are useful for planting cuttings and seeds. And, of course, you will need plants. Bedding plants, available from late spring, are inexpensive - but packets of seeds are even cheaper!

Get yourself a big cardboard box and try to collect together some or all of the following items, in order to make the projects on the following pages: string, nylon thread, peanuts, kitchen foil, acrylic paints and brushes, coloured paper, wooden kebab sticks, lollipop sticks, bamboo poles, scissors, a glue stick, sand, fabric paints, drinking straws, a permanent marker pen, wire coat hangers, fine wire, mosaic tiles and waterproof tile adhesive, rags, fabric scraps, canvas or calico fabric, ribbons, straw and some empty paint cans.

Easy to make

Most projects are simple and straightforward - just follow the instructions and you won't go far wrong! Sometimes you may wish to change things - and that's fine! If the instructions say 'plant pansies' and all you have are some geraniums, then plant the geraniums instead!

You may occasionally need the help of an adult - or at least an adult's permission if, for example, you wish to pick some flowers from the garden!

Naturally Crafty

You may not find a bundle of twigs particularly inspiring – but you'd be surprised what you can make! Collect fallen twigs from the park for a star decoration, or long vine stems from your own back garden for a wreath. On your next trip to the seaside, search the shoreline for driftwood and, while you're at it, see if you can find some seashells. Not any old shells but ones with holes in, so they can be transformed into a pretty outdoor mobile.

Crafty tips
Suitable stems for this project include those from Virginia creeper, Boston ivy, some honeysuckles or a grape vine. Ask a grown-up to help you. The best time to cut the stems is in the autumn, after the leaves have dropped off.

Wreath

Some people like to hang a decorated wreath on their front door at Christmas time. But a simple, undecorated wreath makes an attractive decoration any time of the year. You could even tie on a bunch of dried lavender, to make a scented wreath! But first, you will need to collect some long, flexible stems from a vine or climbing shrub – about 12-15 stems.

1 Start with a long stem, bending it round into a circle and twisting the ends around the circle until they stay in place.

2 Take a second stem, push the thicker end into a gap where you have twisted the ends of the first piece, then wind it round and round the circle, tucking the end into a gap.

3 Add a third stem, then a fourth, and as many more stems as you like.

To make a string of peanuts

Simply thread a large darning needle with string and thread peanuts in their shells on to the string, just as if you were making a necklace. Knot the ends so the peanuts do not slide off! Simply tie to a tree for the birds to eat.

Twig star

Choose three twigs of similar lengths, and bind the ends together with fine wire to make a triangle. Make another triangle, place one on top of the other and bind together where they overlap.

Shell wind chime

You will need:
assortment of shells, with holes
nylon thread
twig or small piece of driftwood
string

1 Cut short lengths of thread and tie firmly on to shells. Tie the other end of each piece to the twig or driftwood.

2 Cut more short lengths of thread, tie one end to the bottom of the first shell, then add another shell. Tie on more shells, until you are pleased with the arrangement. Make sure they are quite close together so they will knock into each other when the wind blows.

3 Tie a length of string to each end of the stick and hang up your shell wind chime in the house or garden, where it will catch the breeze.

Edible Plants from Seed

Growing things to eat can be magic! You plant your seeds, then you stare at the bare earth for days, thinking nothing will happen. Suddenly tiny green shoots poke through – and before you know it you have a crop of plants!

Parsley pot

You will need
parsley pot or large flower pot
gravel, pebbles or broken clay pots
seed compost
parsley seeds

Parsley seeds are tiny and slow to sprout, so you have to be patient. If you can, sow them in a parsley pot – a large flower pot with several planting holes on the sides. Keep parsley well watered and cut it as often as you like – chop it up and add it to vegetables, scrambled eggs, pies, sandwiches, almost any savoury food! And every week or so throughout the summer, keep sowing more seed in your pot, so your supply never runs out!

1 Place a layer of gravel, pebbles or broken clay pots in the base of the pot, then fill with compost to within about 3cm of the rim.

2 Sprinkle the surface of the compost with a thin layer of seeds, then add a little more compost – just enough to cover the seeds lightly.

3 Water until the compost is damp.

Nasturtiums

These are one of the easiest plants to grow from seed. The seeds are larger than most, and easy to handle. Push three or four into a pot of compost in late spring, sprinkle with water and you should see shoots appearing in a few days.

As the plants grow, gently push a few sticks into the soil to give support to the climbing stems. With three sticks tied together at the top, you can make a nasturtium wigwam.

Bottle top bird scarers

To protect seeds and small plants from being eaten by birds, make a bird scarer. Attach pieces of aluminium foil – including milk bottle tops, if you have any – to a length of string suspended above the young plants.

Or why not grow a nasturtium seed in a plastic bottle? Before planting, use a skewer to make a few drainage holes in the base of the bottle, add a layer of gravel to help drainage, then fill with compost.

Water your plants daily and by late summer, you should have mass of leaves and red, orange and yellow flowers. Both leaves and flowers are edible – add them to salads for a peppery flavour.

Painted Pebbles

The next time you go to the beach, look out for some nice, round pebbles to paint. Paint one to make a paperweight, or a whole pocketful to make a snake!

You will need:
round, flat pebbles
acrylic paints
soft paintbrush

Pebble paperweight

1 Firstly, paint your pebble white. You will have to paint one side, then leave it to dry before painting the other side.

2 Now use bright colours to paint a design. The shape of the pebble may suggest what kind of decoration to choose: maybe a flower or a fish?

Crafty tip
Acrylic paints give a hard-wearing finish, but for added protection why not paint your finished pebbles with a coat of water-based varnish?

Pebble snake

1 Paint pebbles white, as before. Leave to dry.

2 Paint each pebble the same, plain colour, then add the squiggles. Add a spot to one pebble as the snake's eye.

3 Arrange pebbles in a wiggly line, with the largest as the snake's head, with progressively smaller pebbles towards the tail.

Sandcastle flags

Playing with sand is fun, whether you are at the beach or in the sandpit. And what better way to adorn a sandcastle than with a selection of home-made paper flags?

To make paper flags

You will need:
selection of coloured paper scraps
felt pens
glue stick
scissors
wooden kebab sticks

1 For the main part of each flag, cut a rectangle measuring 12cm x 7cm. Decorate the flags with felt pens or by gluing on paper cut-outs.

2 Apply a little glue to one of the short edges, place the stick on top and roll the paper round the stick.

Sand play

If you haven't got a bucket and spade, improvise with things you may have in the kitchen. Use a sieve or colander for sifting sand, wooden or plastic cutlery for scooping and scraping and plastic cups for making sand pies!

Toys for Windy Days

A paper windmill is easy to make: stick it in the sand at the beach, or in a flower pot in your garden and watch it spin when the wind blows. A wind sock will show you the direction of the wind – and it's great fun to run along holding the stick, with the colourful ribbon streamers trailing behind you!

To make a windmill

You will need:
tracing paper
thin card
scissors
glass-headed pin
2 plastic drinking straws
cork

B

A

1 Trace off the petal shape from this page and use it as a template to cut seven petal shapes from thin card.

2 Stick the pin through all the card petals at point A.

3 Cut a 1cm length from one of the straws and place it on the pin. Then stick the pin through all petals at point B.

4 Cut another short length from the straw and place it on the pin. Stick the pin point through the top of the other straw, then cut off a small piece of the cork and stick it on the pin point.

To make a
wind sock

You will need:
fabric (see box on right)
scissors
needle and sewing thread
wire
ribbons
string or cord
small metal ring
metal spinner
stick

4 Cut three 35cm lengths of string or cord. Make three holes in the top hem, below the wire, and thread the strings through these holes, tying tightly. Thread the other ends of the three strings through the metal ring and tie firmly, then attach the ring to the spinner.

1 Cut a rectangle of fabric measuring 35cm x 20cm. Stitch the two short ends together, to make a cylinder. Then turn under about 1cm at each end, to form a hem, and stitch.

147

2 Push a length of wire into one of the hems, joining the ends of the wire by twisting them together.

5 Tie a short length of string to the other end of the spinner and tie the string securely to the stick.

3 Cut ribbons into 40cm lengths and stitch to the other hem.

Make a Herb Pot

Most herbs can be cultivated indoors on a windowsill for an all-year-round supply. But in summer, they will thrive outdoors in sunny conditions, so why not plant up a selection in a large container?

1 Put gravel, pebbles or broken clay pots in the base of your container, then fill about two-thirds full with compost.

2 Arrange the herbs on top of the compost. Try to make a balanced arrangement, with the tallest plants such as rosemary, chives or sage in the centre and lower growing types such as parsley, marjoram and oregano around the edges. Thyme, which is very low growing, will tumble over the rim of the pot. Leave gaps between the plants.

3 Keep your herb pot well watered and the plants will grow and thrive and fill the gaps until you have a lovely, scented mass of greenery.

Crafty tips
Keep trimming the plants and use the bits you cut off in cooking.

Lollipop stick plant labels

Every time you have an ice lolly, save the stick. These flat wooden sticks are ideal for labelling plants – especially seeds and bulbs which, once you have put them in the ground, you might easily forget!

To make plant labels

You will need:
lollipop sticks
acrylic paints
paintbrush
permanent marker pen

1 Use paints to decorate one side of each stick with stripes, spots or other patterns.

2 Using the marker pen, write information about the seeds, bulbs or cuttings you have planted, such as the name and date of planting, on the other side.

Marvellous Mosaics

Decorative mosaics have been around for thousands of years. If you make your own, they can't be guaranteed to last that long, but if you are careful, they should withstand all kinds of weather.

To make a mosaic pot

You will need:
spatula
waterproof tile adhesive and grout
terracotta flower pot
vitreous mosaic tiles
rags

Safety

This is a project that needs some adult help. Before you start, unless you wish to use only whole tiles, you will need to ask a grown-up to break the tiles into small pieces. This is best done with a special tool called a tile nipper. After the tiles have been cut, they should be washed to remove any small splinters of glass, and you should wear gloves when you are handling them, as the edges are likely to be sharp.

1 Using the spatula, spread a thick layer of tile grout over the surface of the pot.

2 Press pieces of mosaic tile into the grout, leaving small gaps between each piece.

3 When the whole of the outside of the pot has been covered, leave it to set.

4 Using the spatula again, add more tile grout, pressing it into the gaps between the tiles. With a damp rag, wipe away any excess grout. Leave to set.

5 Use a dry rag to remove any remaining grout from the surface of the tiles.

To make a mosaic number tile

Start with a square of thick plywood or MDF, or a large ceramic tile. Draw a number on the surface, using a waterproof marker pen. Spread tile grout in the area where you have drawn the number and fill with pieces of tile in your chosen colour. Then use whole, unbroken mosaic tiles all round the edge, for a neat border. Spread tile grout over the remaining area and fill in the background with pieces of tile. Leave to dry, then fill in gaps between tiles with more grout, wiping away excess with a damp cloth.

Crafty tips
To stick down the pieces of mosaic and fill in the gaps between, use a combined waterproof tile grout and adhesive, which is available ready mixed in a plastic tub as a thick white paste. It is advisable to wear gloves when handling this adhesive.

Pressed Flowers

H ere's a way to preserve flower heads, petals and leaves collected from the garden, and use them to decorate a card and a bookmark.

To press flowers

You will need:
heavy book
blotting paper or paper kitchen towels
flowers and leaves (see Crafty tip)

1 Open out the book and place a sheet of blotting paper or kitchen paper on one page. Arrange flower heads, petals and leaves over the paper, leaving spaces in between.

Crafty tip
Pick flowers at the end of a dry day. The best types to press are flat flower heads or separate petals. You can also press leaves and stems. Avoid very fat, fleshy flowers, berries and seed pods as these do not dry out successfully and tend to rot and go brown.

2 Place a second piece of paper on top, taking care not to dislodge the flowers and leaves. Close the book. Place it flat with several more books on top and leave for two or three weeks.

3 Check to see if your flowers and leaves have dried out. Open up the book carefully and peel the petals and leaves from the paper. If they are stuck they may not be dry enough and you should leave them for a week or two longer. If, however, they are dry and papery, they are ready to be used.

To make a pressed flower bookmark

You will need:
pressed flowers and leaves
thin card
glue stick
clear self-adhesive plastic film
hole punch
ribbon

1 Arrange pressed flowers and leaves on a strip of thin card. To hold them in place, use a tiny dab of glue.

2 Cut a piece of self-adhesive film about 1cm larger all round than the card. Peel off the backing paper and place the decorated card face down centrally on the sticky side of the film. Trim off any excess film.

3 Punch a hole at the bottom of the bookmark and thread the ribbon through.

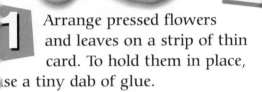

To make a pressed flower card

Fold a rectangle of card in half. Arrange flowers and leaves on the front of the card and stick in place using a glue stick. Cut a piece of clear self-adhesive film slightly smaller than the front of the card, peel off the paper backing and press in place, to seal in the flowers and leaves.

Lovely Lavender

Have you got lavender growing in your garden? It is not only a pretty plant to look at but it is wonderfully perfumed – and butterflies and bees are attracted to it! At the end of the summer, it is a good idea to cut lavender back so it will be encouraged to grow even more flowers next year. Save all the stems that are cut off to make a lavender wand and a lavender sachet.

To make a lavender wand

You will need:
23 lavender stems
1.5 metres narrow ribbon

1 Tie one end of the ribbon around the lavender stems, just below the heads.

2 Just below the point where you have tied the ribbon, bend each stem back over the heads.

3 Holding the bent stems loosely in one hand, take the long end of the ribbon and thread it in and out of the stems. Once you have gone round once, on the next row you will need to go over and under alternate stems, so the ribbon weaves in and out. When this weaving has completely covered the lavender heads, tie the ribbon round the stems and fasten off with a bow.

To make a lavender sachet

155

You will need:
20cm length of very
wide ribbon
sewing thread and needle
dried lavender
(see Crafty tip)
15cm length of narrow ribbon

1 Fold the wide ribbon in
half and stitch up both
sides, to form a bag.

2 Fill the bag with
lavender and tie with
narrow ribbon.

Crafty tip
To dry lavender, tie in
bunches and hang
upside down for a few
weeks, then rub the
flowers off the stems
and store in an
airtight container.

Crafty tip
If you do not have any ribbon, simply use some
scraps of fabric. Sheer, thin fabrics are best, to
allow the lovely lavender scent to come through.

Painted Pots

Why not use paints to decorate a few plain flower pots, transforming them into something bright and beautiful?

To make a painted pot

You will need:
terracotta flower pot
white emulsion paint
acrylic paints
soft paintbrush

1 Unless you want the original clay colour of the pot to show through, first paint the pot white all over.

2 Now add some colour! You could paint the main part of the pot and the rim in different colours, or paint a background colour then add some stripes or another design.

Crafty tips
Painting the pot white to start with will help any subsequent colours to appear nice and bright. Instead of using white acrylic, use emulsion paint, which is a bit cheaper. Ask an adult – they may have some left after decorating the house.

Paint pot hanging basket

Ask a grown-up to save paint pots next time they are decorating. Either 2.5 litre or 5 litre cans of emulsion are best, and they need to be thoroughly washed out before you start.

You will need:
clean, empty emulsion paint cans
acrylic paints
gravel, pebbles or broken
clay pots
potting compost
plants, such as pansies

Painted twig

While you have your paints out, why not paint a twig to act as a plant support or simply to add a splash of colour while you are waiting for flowers to bloom. If the bark is flaky, strip it off before painting your stick.

1 Paint the outside of the cans in a plain colour. Black is a good choice as a single coat should easily cover up any words or pictures printed on the can.

2 When the first coat is dry, mix a bright colour of acrylic paint with a little water to make a runny consistency – but not too runny. Spread the paint thickly along the rim of the can, allowing it to drip down the outside.

3 When the paint is completely dry – and this may take several hours or even overnight – you can plant up your paint pots.

4 Put a layer of gravel, pebbles or broken clay pots in the base of your paint can. Then add compost, about two-thirds full. Add your plants and a little more compost, then hang up your paint can from its handle!

In the Kitchen

Introduction

Eating is such a pleasure – especially when you have prepared the food yourself. Yes, cooking can be great fun and you are never too young to learn how to make delicious, nutritious snacks and meals.

Weights and measures

All measurements are given in ml (millilitres), L (litres), g (grams) and cm (centimetres). Use a weighing scales or measuring jug, where appropriate, and a ruler to measure cake tins. Small measurements are given in tsp (teaspoons) and tbsp (tablespoons).

Try some of the recipes on these pages. There is sure to be something you fancy! How about a delicious dip, a home-made cake, warm from the oven, or even a simple sandwich? Stir up some soup, pack up a picnic, or prepare some great party food.

Just remember to put on your apron first, to protect your clothes, and clear up the kitchen after you have finished!

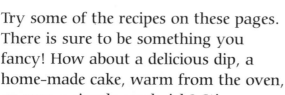

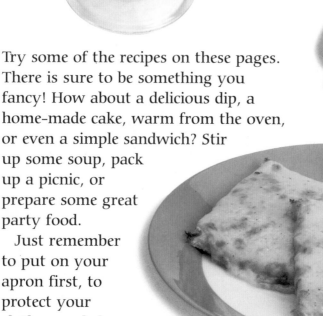

Basic equipment

Here is a list of the tools you will need. You should find most of them in your kitchen.

medium-sized saucepan
rectangular tin, 30cm x 20cm
round cake tin, 20cm diameter
flat baking sheets
measuring spoons
mixing bowl
wooden spoon

- whisk
- weighing scales
- metal skewer
- baking parchment or greaseproof paper
- sieve
- rolling pin

Cooking terms

There may be a few words and phrases you don't understand. Here are some but if you get stuck, a grown-up should have the answer!

- zest – the thinly cut peel of a lemon, orange or lime. Make sure you cut off or grate just the coloured part, not the white, bitter pith underneath.
- eggs – all the recipes on these pages use large sized eggs.
- butter gives a good flavour but you can substitute margarine, which is cheaper.
- plain flour is used for most recipes. Where self-raising flour is needed, you can add baking powder to plain flour. For bread, use a strong flour recommended for bread-making.

Delightful Dippers

Whip up a dip to enjoy with a packet of crisps, some bread or crunchy raw vegetable sticks. It's quick, it's healthy and it's fun!

Salsa

This colourful dip could be served with crisps or corn chips. It also makes a delicious accompaniment to burgers and hot dogs.

You will need:
2 tomatoes
2 spring onions
half a cucumber
2 tbsp tomato relish
2 tbsp tomato ketchup
salt and pepper
fresh coriander, mint or parsley
fresh vegetable sticks, to serve

1 Chop up the tomatoes, spring onions and cucumber as small as you can. Put them in a bowl.

2 Stir in the tomato relish and tomato ketchup, then season with salt and pepper.

3 Snip the fresh herbs into small pieces, using scissors, and stir into the dip just before serving.

Creamy cheese and onion dip

Mix together 2 tbsp each of natural yoghurt, cream cheese and mayonnaise. Add 1 tsp mustard and mix really well with a fork or whisk. Stir in 2 chopped spring onions – or some chopped fresh herbs, if you prefer – and season with salt and pepper. Serve with raw vegetables such as peppers and celery, cut into sticks, or with pitta bread, lightly toasted and cut into fingers.

Avocado dip

This Mexican-style dip, known as guacamole, can be served with corn chips, sometimes known as tortilla chips. Skin two ripe avocados and remove the stones, then mash up the flesh in a bowl. Stir in a tablespoon of tomato relish, two or three chopped spring onions and the juice of a lime. To add a bit of spice, you can add a few drops of chilli sauce, if you want. Stir in some chopped fresh coriander leaves just before serving.

Snack Attack

These recipes are great for a light lunch or supper when you are quite hungry but don't want a big meal. Make enough for one, two or more people!

Salmon fish cakes

This recipe will make six large fish cakes or eight medium-sized ones. Serve the fish cakes with a creamy cheese and onion dip, or with peas or baked beans.

You will need:
4 potatoes
15g butter
2 tbsp milk
200g can of salmon
2 eggs
1 tbsp tomato ketchup
dried breadcrumbs
salt and pepper
2 tbsp oil

1 Peel the potatoes, cut them into even-sized pieces and place in a saucepan with enough cold water to cover. Place on the stove, over high heat, until the water boils, then put on a lid, turn down the heat and cook for about 15 minutes, until soft. Test if the potatoes are done by poking with a skewer. Drain off the water and return the potatoes to the pan.

2 Mash the potatoes, adding the butter and milk. Leave to cool.

3 Drain the salmon and place it in a bowl. Break it up into small pieces with a fork. Add the potato and one of the eggs, the tomato ketchup and some salt and pepper and mix well until thoroughly blended.

4 Divide the mixture into six or eight equal portions. Shape each portion into a cake.

5 Beat the remaining egg in a shallow dish. Put the breadcrumbs in another dish.

6 Dip each fish cake into the egg, so it is coated all over, then into the breadcrumbs.

7 Heat the oil in a frying pan and fry the fish cakes on both sides, until crisp and golden. Drain on kitchen paper before serving.

Alphabet soup

This smooth vegetable soup is made extra filling by adding pasta! Choose tiny pasta shapes such as alphabets or stars, or break spaghetti into short lengths. The soup will serve four people.

You will need:

2 onions
2 celery stalks
25g butter
1 tbsp oil
2 carrots
2 potatoes
2 tomatoes
900ml chicken or vegetable stock
about 100g pasta shapes

1 Peel and chop the onions. Chop the celery. Cook them in the oil and butter in a saucepan over medium heat for about 10 minutes, until soft.

2 Peel and chop the carrots and potatoes and chop the tomatoes, then add to the pan. Cook, stirring, for 2 minutes, then pour in the stock.

3 Increase the heat until the soup starts to boil, then put a lid on the pan, reduce the heat to low and leave to cook for 30 minutes.

4 Allow the soup to cool, then whizz it up, in a blender or food processor, until smooth. Return it to the pan and reheat over medium heat.

5 Cook the pasta in boiling salted water for 3 minutes, or according to the instructions on the packet. Drain and add to the soup.

Cheesy toasts

Grate 75g Cheddar cheese and mix with 2 tsp mustard, 2 tbsp milk and some salt and pepper. Toast two slices of bread under a hot grill, on one side only and spread the cheese mixture over the untoasted sides. Grill until the cheese is golden and bubbly.

Big Breakfast

The first meal of the day – and considered by some people to be the best! Treat yourself to something nourishing and your day will be off to a very good start!

Bacon bangers

Bacon and sausages are breakfast favourites – and they taste twice as nice when they are cooked together, like this! Instructions are given for baking the sausages in the oven but they could be fried or grilled, if you prefer.

You will need:
8 chipolata sausages
8 rashers of streaky bacon
1-2 tbsp oil

1 Heat the oven to gas mark 6/ 200°C/400°F.

2 Stretch the bacon rashers slightly and wrap one around each sausage.

3 Brush a baking tray with oil and arrange the bacon-wrapped bangers on the tray in a single layer. Cook in the oven for 20 minutes, turning them over after 10 minutes. Serve with baked beans and grilled tomatoes.

Boiled egg and soldiers

A boiled egg is simple to cook and very delicious, especially with fingers of buttered toast for dipping! Pour water into a small saucepan so it is deep enough to cover the egg. Place the pan on the stove, over medium–high heat and, just before it starts to boil, carefully place the egg in the water. When the water starts to bubble, start timing! For a large egg, cook for 4 minutes for a set white and a runny yolk. Meanwhile, toast some bread. As soon as the time is up, hold the pan under the cold tap for about 10 seconds, then transfer the egg to an egg cup. Butter the toast and cut it into fingers.

Muesli sundae

Muesli and yoghurt is a healthy
breakfast option – and here's an idea
to make it look and taste extra special!
In a bowl, mix 3 tbsp muesli with 2 tbsp
orange or apple juice and 1 tsp runny honey.
Spoon half this mixture into a sundae glass;
then add a layer of yoghurt. Add the rest of
the muesli and another layer of
yoghurt and top with a
strawberry, or other
fruit, and a sprig of
fresh mint.

Scrambled eggs

To make perfect scrambled eggs for two people,
melt 25g butter in a saucepan over low heat.
Break four eggs into a bowl and add
2 tbsp milk and some salt and pepper.
Stir until well mixed, then add to the
pan. Cook over low heat, stirring all the
time. Be patient, as the eggs will take
about 10 minutes to cook.
You need to stir them so
they do not stick to the
pan, and so you end
up with really
creamy, soft
eggs. You can
stop stirring
just for long
enough to put
some bread in
the toaster or
under the grill.
When the eggs
are ready, divide
them between two
serving plates and
add triangles of
buttered toast.

Brunch Munch

H ere are some ideas for a late breakfast, perfect for a lazy weekend or holiday. Perhaps you could treat your parents to breakfast in bed?

American pancakes

This recipe makes about 12 pancakes – enough for two people or one very greedy one! You can spread the warm pancakes with butter and jam, or serve them in a stack with some maple syrup and a wedge of lemon for squeezing!

You will need:
150g plain flour
1 tsp bicarbonate of soda
1 tsp caster sugar
1 egg
150ml milk
about 25g butter or 1-2 tbsp oil

1 Sift the flour with the bicarbonate of soda into a mixing bowl. Stir in the sugar.

2 Make a hole in the centre of the flour and add the egg. Beat the egg with a wooden spoon or whisk, allowing the flour to gradually become mixed in.

3 Add about a third of the milk and continue beating, allowing more flour to become mixed in.

4 Continue mixing, gradually adding the rest of the milk. When all the flour is incorporated, beat the mixture for about 2 minutes.

5 Place a non-stick or cast iron frying pan over medium heat. Grease lightly with butter or oil. Using a large spoon or ladle, drop small puddles of batter into the pan. After a minute or so, bubbles will appear on the pancakes, then the bubbles will become holes. When these holes appear, the pancakes are ready to be turned over. Do this with a spatula. Cook for a further minute, then remove the pancakes from the pan. Repeat until all the batter has been used up.

Sweetcorn fritters

These can be eaten on their own, or with bacon or beans, and they are absolutely delicious! Instead of canned sweet corn you could use frozen corn which has been allowed to defrost.

You will need:
400g can sweetcorn
1 egg
3-4 tbsp flour
salt and pepper
2 tbsp oil

1 Drain the corn and put it into a mixing bowl. Add the egg and mix well with a wooden spoon.

2 Add the flour and some salt and pepper. Mix well. The mixture should be quite thick, like porridge. If it seems too thin, add a little more flour.

3 Heat the oil in a frying pan over medium heat. Using a large spoon or ladle, drop small puddles of mixture into the pan. Cook for a minute or two, until you can see the edges of the underside of the fritters turning golden brown, then turn them over with a spatula and cook for a further minute or two.

4 Remove the fritters from the pan and repeat until all the mixture has been used up. Serve with baked beans.

Fruit smoothie

In a blender, put a small banana, broken into chunks, and a 150ml carton of natural yoghurt. Fill the empty yoghurt carton with fruit juice – orange, apple or pineapple – and pour into the blender. Then add your choice of fruit – a few raspberries, strawberries or blueberries, perhaps, or a peach or pear peeled and cut into chunks. Whizz until smooth and pour into glasses. This is enough for two or three people.

169

Home-baked Bread

Home-baked bread is fun to make – mixing the dough, kneading it, shaping it into loaves or rolls and watching it magically increase in size! And the smell of it baking is absolutely delicious! This dough can also be adapted to make the pizza recipes on the following pages.

Basic bread dough

You will need:
450g strong white bread flour
2 tsp salt
1 tsp caster sugar
1 sachet of easy blend dried yeast
325ml warm water
1 egg

1 Put the flour, salt, half the sugar and yeast in a large bowl, mix together, then stir in the warm water, using a wooden spoon. The dough should be soft and sticky.

2 Knead the dough on a floured surface for about 5-10 minutes. It should become less sticky and quite springy.

3 Place the dough in a lightly oiled plastic bag, put the bag in a bowl or on a tray and leave in a warm place to rise for about 40 minutes. It should double in size!

4 Knead the dough again, for abou 5 minutes this time. Use it to make a loaf of bread or some rolls, following the instructions opposit

5 Place the loaf or rolls on a baking sheet which has been dusted with flour. Beat together the egg and the remaining sugar with 1 tsp water, and brush over the surface of the dough. Cover with a cloth and leave in a warm place for 30-40 minutes, to rise again.

6 Heat the oven to gas mark 8/ 230°C/450°F. Place the tray of bread or rolls in the oven and bake for 20 minutes (for rolls) or 30 minutes (for a loaf). The bread is ready when it is golden and sounds hollow when you tap it with your knuckles. Transfer to a wire rack and leave to coo

Speckled plait

The recipe for basic bread dough will make two loaves. Cut the dough in half then divide each half into three. Roll and stretch each piece into a long sausage and plait three sausages together. If you don't want to make a plait, just pat the dough into a loaf shape. When you have brushed the dough with the beaten egg mixture, you can sprinkle the top with poppy, sunflower or sesame seeds.

Hedgehog rolls

The recipe for basic bread dough will make 12 rolls. Or you could use half to make a plaited loaf and the other half to make six rolls. Shape the rolls with your hands then, to make them, into hedgehogs, push peppercorns or cloves in place to make eyes, and snip the dough with scissors, to form prickles.

Perfect Pizza

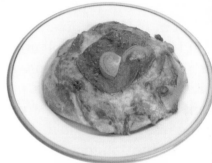

To make pizza bases, follow the recipe for basic bread dough on the previous pages but leave out the sugar and add 2 tbsp olive oil with the water. Knead the dough for 10 minutes, place in an oiled plastic bag in a bowl in a warm place for about 40 minutes, until doubled in size, then follow the pizza recipes below.

Cheesy pizza

The pizza dough, made with 450g flour, will be enough for two pizzas – just right for four hungry people or two very greedy ones! Use the fresh tomato sauce or a jar of ready-made tomato pasta sauce. Instead of mozzarella cheese, you could use Cheddar, Edam, or another cheese.

You will need:
pizza dough (see above)
olive oil
tomato sauce
125g mozzarella cheese
black olives with stones removed
dried oregano
fresh basil leaves

1 Heat the oven to gas mark 8/230°C/450°F. Lightly grease two flat baking trays with olive oil.

2 Take the risen dough from the bag and knead it n a floured surface for –3 minutes.

3 Divide the dough in half and place one half on each tray. Press the dough with your ngers, flattening it out to make two izza bases.

4 Spread each base with about 2-3 tbsp tomato sauce. Cut the cheese into slices and arrange on top, then decorate with olives and sprinkle with oregano.

5 Bake the pizzas for 15 minutes, until the cheese has melted and the edges of the dough are crisp and golden. Sprinkle with fresh basil leaves.

Mini discs

Instead of two medium-sized pizzas, make four smaller ones. Each person could choose their own toppings, such as sliced mushrooms, drained canned tuna or slices of salami.

173

French bread pizza

ut a short baguette in half ngthways and brush the cut surface vith a little olive oil. Add 2 tbsp omato sauce, spreading it evenly over he bread, then add sliced or grated heese. Top with thinly sliced salami nd red pepper and sprinkling f oregano.

ake at gas mark 8/230°C/450°F or 15 minutes. Serve sprinkled with chopped fresh basil.

Faster Pasta

Pasta is quick to cook and satisfyingly filling to eat! Here are some quick and easy ideas to enjoy at snack time, dinner time or party time!

Fresh tomato sauce

This sauce can be used with any pasta or as a pizza topping. The recipe makes enough for four servings and it can be kept in the fridge for up to three days, in a covered container, and reheated when you need it.

You will need:
1 large onion, peeled
2 celery stalks
2 tbsp olive oil
8 ripe tomatoes
4 tbsp tomato purée
4 tbsp water
salt and pepper
fresh basil (optional)

1 Chop the onion and celery into very small pieces. Heat the oil in a saucepan over medium heat and cook the chopped onion and celery for about 10 minutes, stirring frequently, until it is soft and golden.

2 Chop the tomatoes, add them to the pan and cook for a further 2 minutes, then stir in the tomato purée and water.

3 Cook the sauce for a further 10 minutes, then add seasoning.

4 Just before serving, add some chopped fresh basil leaves, if you like.

Easy peasy tuna pasta

This recipe is enough for four people. If you don't like tuna, substitute some chopped, cooked chicken or ham or, for a vegetarian dish, some cheese, cut into cubes.

You will need
250g pasta shells
salt and pepper
150ml carton of single cream
2 tbsp tomato purée
2 tbsp canned sweetcorn
about 12 stuffed green olives
200g can tuna in spring water
tbsp grated Parmesan cheese

1 Boil plenty of water in a large saucepan, adding a pinch of salt. When the water is boiling, add the pasta shells and cook them for 8 minutes, or according to the instructions on the packet.

2 Drain and return the pasta to the saucepan over low heat. Stir in the cream, tomato purée and sweetcorn. Slice the olives and stir these in, too. Add the tuna.

3 Transfer the pasta to a serving dish and sprinkle with Parmesan cheese.

Spaghetti in a hurry

Cook spaghetti according to the instructions on the packet. Cooked meatballs, diced grilled bacon and sliced sausages are all good with spaghetti and delicious with fresh tomato sauce (see recipe on opposite page). Simmer the sauce with the meat gently for about 10 minutes until heated right through and spoon over the drained spaghetti.

Cakes

B̲ake a delicious cake and everyone will want to be invited to tea!

Lemon yoghurt cake

This is a low-fat recipe which makes it healthier than a lot of other cakes – and just as delicious!

1 Heat the oven to gas mark 4/180°C/350°F. Use the vegetable oil to grease a 1.5 litre loaf tin. Line the tin with greaseproof paper or baking parchment.

You will need:
a little vegetable oil
150ml natural yoghurt
grated zest of 1 lemon
250g caster sugar
2 eggs
250g self-raising flour
100g icing sugar
juice of half a lemon

2 Put the yoghurt in a large bowl with the lemon zest and sugar.

3 Break the eggs into a small bowl and, using a wooden spoon, beat them lightly, then add them gradually to the yoghurt mixture, beating all the time. Add the flour and beat again.

4 Pour the mixture into the cake tin and bake for 45 minutes. To test if the cake is done, push a skewer into the centre. If it comes out clean, the cake is ready. If there is some cake mixture sticking to it, return the cake to the oven, bake for a further 5 minutes, and test again.

5 Transfer the cake to a wire rack, peel off the paper and leave to cool.

6 Meanwhile, mix the icing sugar with the lemon juice. Spread over the top of the cooled cake.